On Sales

HARVARD BUSINESS REVIEW PRESS
Boston, Massachusetts

> **HBR Press Quantity Sales Discounts**
>
> Harvard Business Review Press titles are available at significant quantity discounts when purchased in bulk for client gifts, sales promotions, and premiums. Special editions, including books with corporate logos, customized covers, and letters from the company or CEO printed in the front matter, as well as excerpts of existing books, can also be created in large quantities for special needs.
>
> For details and discount information for both print and ebook formats, contact booksales@harvardbusiness.org, tel. 800-988-0886, or www.hbr.org/bulksales.

Copyright 2017 Harvard Business Publishing Corporation
All rights reserved
Printed in the United States of America

No part of this publication may be reproduced, stored in or introduced into a retrieval system, or transmitted, in any form, or by any means (electronic, mechanical, photocopying, recording, or otherwise), without the prior permission of the publisher. Requests for permission should be directed to permissions@hbsp.harvard.edu, or mailed to Permissions, Harvard Business School Publishing, 60 Harvard Way, Boston, Massachusetts 02163.

The web addresses referenced in this book were live and correct at the time of the book's publication but may be subject to change.

Library of Congress Cataloging-in-Publication Data

Names: Zoltners, Andris A., interviewee.
Title: HBR's 10 must reads on sales : with bonus interview of Andris Zoltners.
Other titles: On sales : with bonus interview of Andris Zoltners | HBR's 10 must reads (Series)
Description: Boston, Massachusetts : Harvard Business Review Press, [2017] | Series: HBR's 10 must reads series
Identifiers: LCCN 2016051347 | ISBN 9781633694538
Subjects: LCSH: Sales management.
Classification: LCC HF5438.4 .H395 2017 | DDC 658.8/1—dc23 LC record available at https://lccn.loc.gov/2016051347

ISBN: 978-1-63369-453-8
eISBN:978-1-63369-328-9

Contents

Major Sales: Who *Really* Does the Buying? 1
by Thomas V. Bonoma

Ending the War Between Sales and Marketing 23
by Philip Kotler, Neil Rackham, and Suj Krishnaswamy

Match Your Sales Force Structure to Your Business Life Cycle 45
by Andris A. Zoltners, Prabhakant Sinha, and Sally E. Lorimer

The End of Solution Sales 67
by Brent Adamson, Matthew Dixon, and Nicholas Toman

Selling into Micromarkets 83
by Manish Goyal, Maryanne Q. Hancock, and Homayoun Hatami

Dismantling the Sales Machine 101
by Brent Adamson, Matthew Dixon, and Nicholas Toman

Tiebreaker Selling 115
by James C. Anderson, James A. Narus, and Marc Wouters

Making the Consensus Sale 127
by Karl Schmidt, Brent Adamson, and Anna Bird

The Right Way to Use Compensation 139
by Mark Roberge

How to *Really* Motivate Salespeople 149
by Doug J. Chung

BONUS
Getting Beyond "Show Me the Money" 161
An interview with Andris Zoltners by Daniel McGinn

About the Contributors 169
Index 171

On
Sales

Major Sales

Who Really Does the Buying? **by Thomas V. Bonoma**

> *You don't understand: Willy was a salesman. . . . He don't put a bolt to a nut. He don't tell you the law or give you medicine. He's a man way out there in the blue, riding on a smile and a shoeshine. And when they start not smiling back—that's an earthquake.*
>
> —Arthur Miller, *Death of a Salesman*

MANY COMPANIES' SELLING EFFORTS are models of marketing efficiency. Account plans are carefully drawn, key accounts receive special management attention, and substantial resources are devoted to the sales process, from prospect identification to postsale service. Even such well-planned and well-executed selling strategies often fail, though, because management has an incomplete understanding of buying psychology—the human side of selling. Consider the following two examples:

- A fast-growing maker and seller of sophisticated graphics computers had trouble selling to potentially major customers. Contrary to the industry practice of quoting high list prices and giving large discounts to users who bought in quantity, this company priced 10% to 15% lower than competitors and gave smaller quantity discounts. Even though its net price was often the lowest, the company met resistance from buyers. The reason, management later learned, was that purchasing agents measured themselves and were measured by their superiors less by the net price of the sophisticated computers they bought than by the amount deducted from the price during negotiations. The discount had a significance to buyers that sound pricing logic could not predict.

- Several years ago, at AT&T's Long Lines division, an account manager was competing against a vendor with possibly better technology who threatened to lure away a key account. Among the customer's executives who might make the final decision about whether to switch from Bell were a telecommunications manager who had once been a Bell employee, a vice president of data processing who was known as a "big-name system buster" in his previous job because he had replaced all the IBM computers with other vendors' machines, and an aggressive telecommunications division manager who seemed to be unreachable by the AT&T team.

  AT&T's young national account manager was nearly paralyzed by the threat. His team had never seriously considered the power, motivations, or perceptions of the various executives in the customer company, which had been buying from AT&T for many years. Without such analysis, effective and coordinated action on short notice—the usual time available for response to sales threats—was impossible.

Getting at the Human Factors

How can psychology be used to improve sales effectiveness? My contention is that seller awareness of and attention to the human factors in purchasing will produce higher percentages of completed sales and fewer unpleasant surprises in the selling process.

It would be inaccurate to call the human side of selling an emerging sales concern; only the most advanced companies recognize the psychology of buying as a major factor in improving account selection and selling results. Yet in most industries, the bulk of a company's business comes from a small minority of its customers. Retaining these key accounts is getting increasingly difficult

Idea in Brief

When is a buyer not really a buyer? How can the best product at the lowest price turn off buyers? Are there anonymous leaders who make the actual buying decisions? As these questions suggest, the reality of buying and selling is often not what it seems. What's more, salespeople often overlook the psychological and emotional factors that figure strongly in buying and selling. By failing to observe these less tangible aspects of selling, a vendor can lose sales without understanding why.

In this article, first published in 1982, Bonoma sets up a procedure for analyzing buying decisions and tells sellers how to apply the resulting framework to specific situations. Steps in the procedure include the following:

- **Identifying the actual decision makers.** Though it may come as a surprise, power does not correlate perfectly with organizational rank. The author outlines five bases of power and offers six behavioral clues for identifying the real decision makers.

- **Determining how buyers view their self-interest.** All buyers act selfishly, but they sometimes miscalculate. As a result, diagnosing motivation is one of the most difficult management tasks to do accurately. The author suggests several techniques to determine how buyers choose their own self-interest.

- **Gathering and applying psychological intelligence.** There is no formula for placing sound psychological analyses magically in the sales staff's hands. However, the author offers three guidelines—make sure that sales calls are highly productive and informative, listen to the sales force, and reward rigorous fact gathering, analysis, and execution—to help managers increase sales effectiveness.

as buyers constantly look not only for the best deal but also for the vendor that best understands them and their needs. It is this understanding and the targeted selling that results from it that can most benefit marketing managers.

Buying a corporate jet

The personal aspects and their complexities become apparent when one looks closely at an example of the buying process: the purchase of a business jet, which carries a price tag in excess of $3 million. The business-jet market splits obviously into two segments: those companies that already own or operate a corporate aircraft and those that do not.

In the owner market, the purchase process may be initiated by the chief executive officer, a board member (wishing to increase efficiency or security), the company's chief pilot, or through vendor efforts like advertising or a sales visit. The CEO will be central in deciding whether to buy the jet, but he or she will be heavily influenced by the company's pilot, financial officer, and perhaps by the board itself.

Each party in the buying process has subtle roles and needs. The salesperson who tries to impress, for example, both the CEO with depreciation schedules and the chief pilot with minimum runway statistics will almost certainly not sell a plane if he overlooks the psychological and emotional components of the buying decision. "For the chief executive," observes one salesperson, "you need all the numbers for support, but if you can't find the kid inside the CEO and excite him or her with the raw beauty of the new plane, you'll never sell the equipment. If you sell the excitement, you sell the jet."

The chief pilot, as an equipment expert, often has veto power over purchase decisions and may be able to stop the purchase of one or another brand of jet by simply expressing a negative opinion about, say, the plane's bad weather capabilities. In this sense, the pilot not only influences the decision but also serves as an information gatekeeper by advising management on the equipment to select. Though the corporate legal staff will formulate the purchase agreement and the purchasing department will acquire the jet, these parties may have little to say about whether or how the plane will be obtained, and which type. The users of the jet—middle and upper management of the buying company, important customers, and others—may have at least an indirect role in choosing the equipment.

The involvement of many people in the purchase decision creates a group dynamic that the selling company must factor into its sales planning. Who makes up the buying group? How will the parties interact? Who will dominate and who submit? What priorities do the individuals have?

It takes about three months for those companies that already own or operate aircraft to reach a decision. Because even the most successful vendor will sell no more than 90 jets a year, every serious prospect is a key account. The non-owners, not surprisingly, represent an even more complex market, since no precedent or aviation specialists exist.

The buying process for other pieces of equipment and for services will be more or less similar, depending on the company, product, and people involved. The purchase of computer equipment, for example, parallels the jet decision, except that sales prospects are likely to include data processing and production executives and the market is divided into small and large prospects rather than owners and nonowners. In other cases (such as upgrading the corporate communications network, making a fleet purchase, or launching a plant expansion), the buying process may be very different. Which common factors will reliably steer selling-company management toward those human considerations likely to improve selling effectiveness?

Different buying psychologies exist that make effective selling difficult. On the one hand, companies don't buy, people do. This knowledge drives the seller to analyze who the important buyers are and what they want. On the other hand, many individuals, some of whom may be unknown to the seller, are involved in most major purchases. Even if all the parties are identified, the outcome of their interaction may be unpredictable from knowledge of them as individuals. Effective selling requires usefully combining the individual and group dynamics of buying to predict what the buying "decision-making unit" will do. For this combination to be practical, the selling company must answer four key questions.

Question 1: Who's in the Buying Center?

The set of roles, or social tasks, buyers can assume is the same regardless of the product or participants in the purchase decision. This set of roles can be thought of as a fixed set of behavioral pigeonholes into which different managers from different functions can be placed to aid understanding. Together, the buying managers who take on these roles can be thought of as a "buying center."[1]

The exhibit "Members of the buying center and their roles" shows six buying roles encountered in every selling situation. I have illustrated these roles using the purchase or upgrading of a telecommunications system as an example. Let's consider each triangle, representing a buying role, in turn.

The *initiator* of the purchase process, whether for a jet, paper towels, or communication services, recognizes that some company problem can be solved or avoided by acquiring a product or service. A company's turboprop aircraft may provide neither the speed nor the range to get top management quickly to and from scattered operations. The prospective buyer of communications equipment may want to take advantage of technological improvements or to reduce costs through owning instead of leasing.

One or more *gatekeepers* are involved in the purchase process. These individuals, who may have the title of buyer or purchasing manager, usually act as problem or product experts. They are paid to keep up on the range of vendor offerings. In the jet example, the chief pilot will ordinarily fill this role. In the telecommunications example given in the exhibit, corporate purchasing, the corporate telecommunications staff, or, increasingly, data-processing experts may be consulted. By controlling (literally keeping the gate open or shut for) information and, sometimes, vendor access to corporate decision makers, the gatekeepers largely determine which vendors get the chance to sell. For some purchases the gatekeeping process is formalized through the use of an approved-vendors list, which constitutes a written statement of who can (and who, by absence, cannot) sell to the company.

Influencers are those who have a say in whether a purchase is made and about what is bought. The range of influencers becomes increasingly broad as major purchases are contemplated, because so many corporate resources are involved and so many people affected. In important decisions, board committees, stockholders of a public company, and even "lowly" mechanics can become influencers. One mining-machinery company encountered difficulty selling a new type of machine to its underground-mining customers. It turned out that mine maintenance personnel, who influenced the buying

Members of the buying center and their roles

Initiator	Division general manager proposes to replace the company's telecommunications system
Decider	Vice president of administration selects, with influence from others, the vendor the company will deal with and the system it will buy
Influencers	Corporate telecommunications department and the vice president of data processing have important say about which system and vendor the company will deal with
Purchaser	Corporate purchasing department completes the purchase to specifications by negotiating or bidding
Gatekeeper	Corporate purchasing and corporate telecommunications departments analyze the company's needs and recommend likely matches with potential vendors
Users	All division employees who use the telecommunications equipment

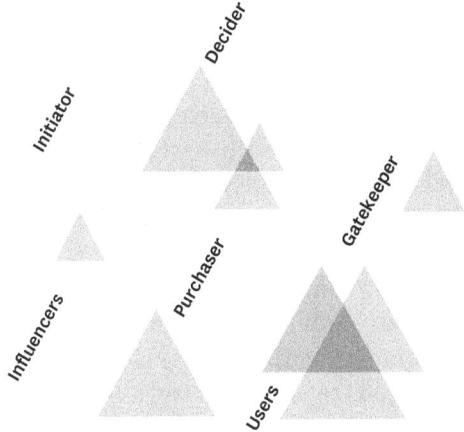

decision, resisted the purchase because they would have to learn to fix the new machine and maintain another stock of spare parts.

The *deciders* are those who say yes or no to the contemplated purchase. Often with major purchases, many of a company's senior managers act together to carry out the decider role. Ordinarily, however, one of these will become champion or advocate of the contemplated purchase and move it to completion. Without such a champion, many purchases would never be made. It is important to point out that deciders often do not sign off on purchases, nor do they make them. That is left to others. Though signers often represent themselves as deciders, such representation can be deceptive. It is possible for a vendor with a poor feel for the buying center never to become aware of the real movers in the buying company.

The purchase of executive computer workstations clearly illustrates both the importance of the champion and the behind-the-scenes role of the decider. A high-level executive who has become interested in using computers at his or her job after reading a magazine article or after tinkering with a home computer might decide to try out microcomputers or time-sharing terminals. The executive might then ask the company's data-processing group—which is likely to be quite resistant and averse to executive meddling—to evaluate available microcomputer equipment. When trial purchases are made, the high-level executive will quietly help steer the system through the proper channels leading to acceptance and further purchases. The vendor, dealing directly with the data-processing people, may never be aware that this decider exists.

The *purchaser* and the *user* are those concerned, respectively, with obtaining and consuming the product or service. The corporate purchasing department usually fills the purchaser role. Who fills the user role depends on the product or service.

Remember that I am discussing social roles, not individuals or groups of individuals. As such, the number of managers filling the buying roles varies from one to 35. In very trivial situations, such as a manager's purchase of a pocket calculator on a business trip, one person will fill all six roles. The triangles in the exhibit would overlap: the manager initiates (perceives a need), "gatekeeps" (what brand did I forget at home?), influences himself or herself (this is more than I need, but it's only $39.95), decides, buys, and uses the equipment.

In more important buying situations, the number of managers assuming roles increases. In a study of 62 capital equipment and service acquisitions in 31 companies, Wesley J. Johnston and I quantified the buying center.[2] In the typical capital equipment purchase, an average of four departments (engineering and purchasing were always included), three levels of management hierarchy (for example, manager, regional manager, vice president), and seven different persons filled the six buying roles. For services, the corresponding numbers were four departments, two levels of management, and five managers. As might be expected, the more complex and involved the buying decision, the larger the decision unit and the more careful its decisions. For example, when packing supplies were ordered, little vendor searching or postsale evaluation was involved. When a new boiler was bought, careful vendor comparisons and postsale audits were undertaken.

Question 2: Who Are the Powerful Buyers?

As useful as the buying-center concept is, it is difficult to apply because managers do not wear tags that say "decision maker" or "unimportant person."[3] The powerful are often invisible, at least to vendor representatives.

Unfortunately, power does not correlate perfectly with organizational rank. As the case of the mine maintenance personnel illustrates, those with little formal power may be able to stop a purchase or hinder its completion. A purchasing manager who will not specify a disfavored vendor or the secretary who screens one vendor's salespeople because of a real or imagined slight also can dramatically change the purchasing outcome. Sales efforts cannot be directed through a simple reading of organizational charts; the selling company must identify the powerful buying-center members.

In the exhibit "Bases of power," I outline five major power bases in the corporation. In addition, I have categorized them according

Bases of power

Type of power	Champion	Veto
Reward Ability to provide monetary, political, or psychological rewards to others for compliance	n	
Coercive Ability to provide monetary or other punishments for noncompliance	n	
Attraction Ability to elicit compliance from others because they like you	n	n
Expert Ability to elicit compliance because of technical expertise, either actual or reputed		n
Status Compliance-gaining ability derived from a legitimate position of power in a company		n

Note: These five power bases were originally proposed over 20 years ago by psychologists J.R.P. French, Jr., and Bertram Raven. See "The Bases of Social Power" in D. Cartwright, ed., *Studies in Social Power* (University of Michigan Press, 1959).

to whether their influence is positive (champion power) or negative (veto power).

Reward power refers to a manager's ability to encourage purchases by providing others with monetary, social, political, or psychological benefits. In one small company, for instance, the marketing vice president hoped to improve marketing decisions by equipping the sales force with small data-entry computers. Anticipating objections that the terminals were unnecessary, she felt forced to offer the sales vice president a computer of his own. The purchase was made.

Coercive power refers to a manager's ability to impose punishment on others. Of course, threatening punishment is not the same thing as having the power to impose it. Those managers who wave sticks most vigorously are sometimes the least able to deliver anything beyond a gentle breeze.

Attraction power refers to a person's ability to charm or otherwise persuade people to go along with his or her preferences. Next to the ability to reward and punish, attraction is the most potent power base in managerial life. Even CEOs find it difficult to rebut a key customer with whom they have flown for ten years who says, "Joe, as your friend, I'm telling you that buying this plane would be a mistake."

When a manager gets others to go along with his judgment because of real or perceived expertise in some area, *expert power* is being invoked. A telecommunications manager will find it difficult to argue with an acknowledged computer expert who contends that buying a particular telephone switching system is essential for the "office of the future"—or that not buying it now eventually will make effective communication impossible. With expert power, the skills need not be real, if by "real" we mean that the individual actually possesses what is attributed to him. It is enough that others believe that the expert has special skills or are willing to respect his opinion because of accomplishments in a totally unrelated field.

Status power comes from having a high position in the corporation. This notion of power is most akin to what is meant by the word "authority." It refers to the kind of influence a president has over a first-line supervisor and is more restricted than the other power bases. At first glance, status power might be thought of as similar to reward or coercive power. But it differs in significant ways. First, the major influence activity of those positions of corporate authority is persuasion, not punishment or reward. We jawbone rather than dangle carrots and taunt with sticks because others in the company also have significant power that they could invoke in retaliation.

Second, the high-status manager can exercise his or her status repeatedly only because subordinates allow it. In one heavy-manufacturing division, for example, the continual specification of favored suppliers by a plant manager (often at unfavorable prices) led to a "palace revolt" among other managers whose component cost evaluations were constantly made to look poor. Third, the power base of those in authority is very circumscribed since authority only tends to work in a downward direction on the organization chart and is restricted to specific work-related requests. Status power is one of the weaker power bases.

Buying centers and individual managers usually display one dominant power base in purchasing decisions. In one small company, an important factor is whether the manager arguing a position is a member of the founding family—a kind of status power and attraction power rolled into one. In a large high-technology defense contractor, almost all decisions are made on the basis of real or reputed expertise. This is true even when the issue under consideration has nothing to do with hardware or engineering science.

The key to improved selling effectiveness is in observation and investigation to understand prospects' corporate power culture. The sales team must also learn the type of power key managers in the buying company have or aspire to. Discounts or offers of price reductions may not be especially meaningful to a young turk in the buying company who is most concerned with status power; a visit by senior selling-company management may prove much more effective for flattering the ego and making the sale. Similarly, sales management may wish to make more technical selling appeals to engineers or other buying-company staff who base their power on expertise.

The last two columns of the exhibit show that the type of power invoked may allow the manager to support or to oppose a proposal, but not always both. I believe status and expert power are more often employed by their holders to veto decisions with which they do not agree. Because others are often "sold" on the contemplated purchase, vetoing it generally requires either the ability to perceive aspects not seen by the average manager because of special expertise or the broader view that high corporate status is said to provide. Reward and coercive power are more frequently used to push through purchases and the choice of favored vendors. Attraction power seems useful and is used by both champions and vetoers. The central point here is that for many buying-center members, power tends to be unidirectional.

Six behavioral clues

On the basis of the preceding analysis of power centers, I have distilled six clues for identifying the powerful:

1. Though power and formal authority often go together, the correlation between the two is not perfect. The selling company must take into account other clues about where the true buying power lies.

2. One way to identify buying-center power holders is to observe communications in the buying company. Of course, the powerful are not threatened by others, nor are they often promised rewards. Still, even the most powerful managers are likely to be influenced by others, especially by those whose power is based on attraction or expertise. Those with less power use persuasion and rational argument to try to influence the more powerful. Managers to whom others direct much attention but who receive few offers of rewards or threats of punishment usually possess substantial decision-making power.

3. Buying-center decision makers may be disliked by those with less power. Thus, when others express concern about one buying-center member's opinions along with their feelings of dislike or ambivalence, sellers have strong clues as to who the powerful buyer is.

4. High-power buyers tend to be one-way information centers, serving as focal points for information from others. The vice president who doesn't come to meetings but who receives copies of all correspondence about a buying matter is probably a central influencer or decider.

5. The most powerful buying-center members are probably not the most easily identified or the most talkative members of their groups. Indeed, the really powerful buying group members often send others to critical negotiations because they are confident that little of substance will be made final without their approval.

6. No correlation exists between the functional area of a manager and his or her power within a company. It is not possible to approach the data-processing department blindly to find decision makers for a new computer system, as many sellers of mainframes have learned. Nor can one simply look to the CEO to find a decision maker for a corporate plane. There is no substitute for working hard to understand the dynamics of the buying company.

Question 3: What Do They Want?

Diagnosing motivation accurately is one of the easiest management tasks to do poorly and one of the most difficult to do well. Most managers have lots of experience at diagnosing another's wants, but though the admission comes hard, most are just not very accurate when trying to figure out what another person wants and will do. A basic rule of motivation is as follows: All buyers (indeed, all people) act selfishly or try to be selfish but sometimes miscalculate and don't serve their own interests. Thus, buyers attempt to maximize their gains and minimize their losses from purchase situations. How do buyers choose their own self-interest? The following are insights into that decision-making process from research.

First, buyers act as if a complex product or service were decomposable into various benefits. Examples of benefits might include product features, price, reliability, and so on.

Second, buyers segment the potential benefits into various categories. The most common of these are financial, product-service, social-political, and personal. For some buyers, the financial benefits are paramount, while for others, the social-political ones—how others in the company will view the purchase—rank highest. Of course, the dimensions may be related, as when getting the lowest-cost product (financial) results in good performance evaluations and a promotion (social-political).

Finally, buyers ordinarily are not certain that purchasing the product will actually bring the desired benefit. For example, a control computer sold on its reliability and industrial-strength construction may or may not fulfill its promise. Because benefits have value only if they actually are delivered, the buyer must be confident that the selling company will keep its promises. Well-known vendors, like IBM or Xerox, may have some advantage over lesser-known companies in this respect.

As marketers know, not all promised benefits will be equally desired by all customers. All buyers have top-priority benefit classes, or "hot buttons." For example, a telecommunications manager weighing a choice between Bell and non-Bell equipment will find some benefits, like ownership, available only from non-Bell vendors. Other desired benefits, such as reputation for service and reliability, may be available to a much greater degree from Bell. The buyer who has financial priorities as a hot button may decide to risk possible service-reliability problems for the cost-reduction benefits available through ownership. Another manager—one primarily concerned with reducing the social-political risks that result from service problems—may reach a different decision. The exhibit "Dominant motives for buying a telecommunications system" schematically

Dominant motives for buying a telecommunications system

The benefits in the shaded column are more highly valued than the others and represent the company's "hot button."

Benefit class

Financial	Product or service	Social or political	Personal
Absolute cost savings	Pre- and postsales service	Will purchase enhance the buyer's standing with the buying team or top management?	Will purchase increase others' liking or respect for the buyer?
Cheaper than competitive offerings	Specific features		
	Space occupied by unit		How does purchase fit with buyer's self-concept?
Will provide operating-cost reductions	Availability		
Economics of leasing versus buying			

shows the four classes into which buyers divide benefits. The telecommunications example illustrates each class.

Outlining the buyer's motivation suggests several possible selling approaches. The vendor can try to focus the buyer's attention on benefits not a part of his or her thinking. A magazine sales representative, for instance, devised a questionnaire to help convince an uncertain client to buy advertising space. The questionnaire sought information about the preferred benefits—in terms of reach, audience composition, and cost per thousand readers. When the prospective buyer "played this silly game" and filled out the questionnaire, he convinced himself of the superior worth of the vendor's magazine on the very grounds he was seeking to devalue it.

Conversely, sellers can de-emphasize the buyer's desire for benefits on which the vendor's offering stacks up poorly. For example, if a competing vendor's jet offers better fuel economy, the selling company might attempt to refocus the buyer's attention toward greater speed or lower maintenance costs.

The vendor can also try to increase the buyer's confidence that promised benefits will be realized. One software company selling legal administrative systems, for example, provides a consulting service that remote users can phone if they are having problems, backup copies of its main programs in case users destroy the original, a complete set of input forms to encourage full data entry, and regular conferences to keep users current on system revisions. These services are designed to bolster the confidence of extremely conservative administrators and lawyers who are shopping for a system.

Finally, vendors often try to change what the buyer wants or which class of benefits he or she responds to most strongly. My view of motivation suggests that such an approach is almost always unsuccessful. Selling strategy needs to work with the buyer's motivations, not around them.

Question 4: How Do They Perceive Us?

How buyers perceive the selling company, its products, and its personnel is very important to efficient selling. Powerful buyers invariably have a wide range of perceptions about a vending company.

One buyer will have a friend at another company who has used a similar product and claimed that "it very nearly ruined us." Another may have talked to someone with a similar product who claims that the vending company "even sent a guy out on a plane to Hawaii to fix the unit there quickly. These people really care."

One drug company representative relates the story of how the company was excluded from all the major metropolitan hospitals in one city because a single influential physician believed that one of the company's new offerings was implicated in a patient's death. This doctor not only generalized his impressions to include all the company's products but encouraged his friends to boycott the company.

A simple scheme for keeping tabs on how buyers perceive sellers is to ask sales officials to estimate how the important buyers judge the vending company and its actions. This judgment can be recorded on a continuum ranging from negative to positive. If a more detailed judgment is desired, the selling company can place its products and its people on two axes perpendicular to each other, like this:

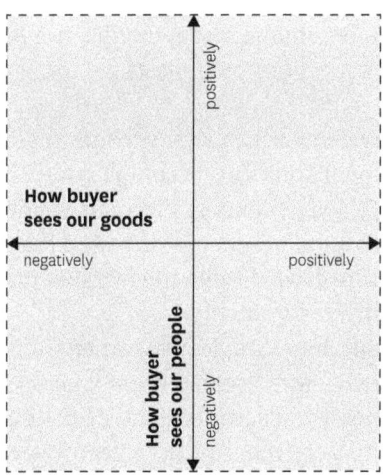

The scarcity of marketing dollars and the effectiveness of champions in the buying process argue strongly for focusing resources where they are likely to do the most good. Marketing efforts should aim at those in the buying company who like the selling company, since they are partially presold. While there is no denying the adage, "It's important to sell everybody," those who diffuse their efforts this way often sell no one.

Gathering Psychological Intelligence

While I would like to claim that some new technique will put sound psychological analyses magically in your sales staff's hands, no such formula exists. But I have used the human-side approach in several companies to increase sales effectiveness, and there are only three guidelines needed to make it work well.

Make productive sales calls a norm, not an oddity

Because of concern about the rapidly rising cost of a sales call, managers are seeking alternative approaches to selling. Sales personnel often do not have a good idea of why they are going on most calls, what they hope to find out, and which questions will give them the needed answers. Sales-call planning is not only a matter of minimizing miles traveled or courtesy calls on unimportant prospects but of determining what intelligence is needed about key buyers and what questions or requests are likely to produce that information.

I recently traveled with a major account representative of a duplication equipment company, accompanying him on the five calls he made during the day. None of the visits yielded even 10% of the potential psychological or other information that the representative could use on future calls, despite the fact that prospects made such information available repeatedly.

At one company, for example, we learned from a talkative administrator that the CEO was a semi-recluse who insisted on approving equipment requests himself; that one of the divisional managers had (without the agreement of the executive who was our host) brought in a competitor's equipment to test; and that a new duplicator the vendor had sold to the company was more out of service than in. The salesperson pursued none of this freely offered information, nor did he think any of it important enough to write down or pass on to the sales manager. The call was wasted because the salesperson didn't know what he was looking for or how to use what was offered him.

The exhibit "Matrix for gathering psychological information" shows a matrix that can be used to capture on a single sheet of paper essential psychological data about a customer. I gave some clues for filling in the matrix earlier in the article, but how sales representatives go about gathering the information depends on the industry, the product, and especially the customer. In all cases, however, key selling assessments involve (1) isolating the powerful buying-center members, (2) identifying what they want in terms of both their hot buttons and specific needs, and (3) assessing their perceptions of the situation. Additionally, gathering psychological information is more often a matter of listening carefully than of asking clever questions during the sales interview.

Listen to the sales force

Nothing discourages intelligence gathering as much as the sales force's conviction that management doesn't really want to hear what salespeople know about an account. Many companies require the sales force to file voluminous call reports and furnish other data—which vanish, never to be seen or even referred to again unless a sales representative is to be punished for one reason or another.

To counter this potentially fatal impediment, I recommend a sales audit. Evaluate all sales force control forms and call reports and discard any that have not been used by management for planning or control purposes in the last year. This approach has a marvelously uplifting effect all around; it frees the sales force from filling in forms it knows nobody uses, sales management from gathering forms it doesn't know what to do with, and data processing from processing reports no one ever requests. Instead, use a simple, clear, and accurate sales control form of the sort suggested in the matrix exhibit—preferably on a single sheet of paper for a particular sales period. These recommendations may sound drastic, but where

Matrix for gathering psychological information

Who's in the buying center, and what is the base of their power?

_____

_____

_____

Who are the powerful buyers, and what are their priorities?

_____

_____

_____

What specific benefits does each important buyer want?

_____

_____

_____

How do the important buyers see us?

_____

_____

_____

Selling strategy

_____

_____

_____

management credibility in gathering and using sales force intelligence is absent, drastic measures may be appropriate.

Emphasize homework and details
Having techniques for acquiring sales intelligence and attending to reports is not enough. Sales management must stress that yours is a company that rewards careful fact gathering, tight analysis, and impeccable execution. This message is most meaningful when it comes from the top.

Cautionary Notes

The group that influences a purchase doesn't call itself a buying center. Nor do decision makers and influencers think of themselves in those terms. Managers must be careful not to mistake the analysis and ordering process for the buyers' actions themselves. In addition, gathering data such as I have recommended is a sensitive issue. For whatever reasons, it is considered less acceptable to make psychological estimates of buyers than economic ones. Computing the numbers without understanding the psychology, however, leads to lost sales. Finally, the notion implicit throughout this article has been that sellers must understand buying, just as buyers must understand selling. When that happens, psychology and marketing begin to come together usefully. Closed sales follow almost as an afterthought.

Originally published in July–August 2006. Reprint R0607P

Notes
1. The concept of the buying center was proposed in its present form by Frederick E. Webster, Jr., and Yoram Wind in *Organizational Buying Behavior* (Prentice-Hall, 1972).
2. Wesley J. Johnston and Thomas V. Bonoma, "Purchase Process for Capital Equipment and Services," *Industrial Marketing Management,* vol. 10, 1981.
3. In the interest of saving space, I will not substantiate each reference to psychological research. Documentation for my assertions can be found in Thomas V. Bonoma and Gerald Zaltman, *Management Psychology* (Kent Publishing, 1981). See chapter 8 for the power literature and chapter 3 for material on motivation.

Ending the War Between Sales and Marketing

by Philip Kotler, Neil Rackham, and Suj Krishnaswamy

PRODUCT DESIGNERS LEARNED YEARS AGO that they'd save time and money if they consulted with their colleagues in manufacturing rather than just throwing new designs over the wall. The two functions realized it wasn't enough to just coexist—not when they could work together to create value for the company and for customers. You'd think that marketing and sales teams, whose work is also deeply interconnected, would have discovered something similar. As a rule, though, they're separate functions within an organization, and, when they do work together, they don't always get along. When sales are disappointing, Marketing blames the sales force for its poor execution of an otherwise brilliant rollout plan. The sales team, in turn, claims that Marketing sets prices too high and uses too much of the budget, which instead should go toward hiring more salespeople or paying the sales reps higher commissions. More broadly, sales departments tend to believe that marketers are out of touch with what's really going on with customers. Marketing believes the sales force is myopic—too focused on individual customer experiences, insufficiently aware of the larger market, and blind to the future. In short, each group often undervalues the other's contributions.

This lack of alignment ends up hurting corporate performance. Time and again, during research and consulting assignments, we've seen both groups stumble (and the organization suffer) because they were out of sync. Conversely, there is no question that, when

Sales and Marketing work well together, companies see substantial improvement on important performance metrics: Sales cycles are shorter, market-entry costs go down, and the cost of sales is lower. That's what happened when IBM integrated its sales and marketing groups to create a new function called Channel Enablement. Before the groups were integrated, IBM senior executives Anil Menon and Dan Pelino told us, Sales and Marketing operated independent of one another. Salespeople worried only about fulfilling product demand, not creating it. Marketers failed to link advertising dollars spent to actual sales made, so Sales obviously couldn't see the value of marketing efforts. And, because the groups were poorly coordinated, Marketing's new product announcements often came at a time when Sales was not prepared to capitalize on them.

Curious about this kind of disconnect between Sales and Marketing, we conducted a study to identify best practices that could help enhance the joint performance and overall contributions of these two functions. We interviewed pairs of chief marketing officers and sales vice presidents to capture their perspectives. We looked in depth at the relationship between Sales and Marketing in a heavy equipment company, a materials company, a financial services firm, a medical systems company, an energy company, an insurance company, two high-tech electronic products companies, and an airline. Among our findings:

- The marketing function takes different forms in different companies at different product life-cycle stages—all of which can deeply affect the relationship between Sales and Marketing.

- The strains between Sales and Marketing fall into two main categories: economic and cultural.

- It's not difficult for companies to assess the quality of the working relationship between Sales and Marketing. (This article includes a diagnostic tool for doing so.)

- Companies can take practical steps to move the two functions into a more productive relationship, once they've established where the groups are starting from.

Idea in Brief

Sales departments tend to believe that marketers are out of touch with what's really going on in the marketplace. Marketing people, in turn, believe the sales force is myopic—too focused on individual customer experiences, insufficiently aware of the larger market, and blind to the future. In short, each group undervalues the other's contributions. Both stumble (and organizational performance suffers) when they are out of sync. Yet few firms seem to make serious overtures toward analyzing and enhancing the relationship between these two critical functions.

Curious about the misalignment between Sales and Marketing, the authors interviewed pairs of chief marketing officers and sales vice presidents to capture their perspectives. They looked in depth at the relationship between Sales and Marketing in a variety of companies in different industries. Their goal was to identify best practices that could enhance the joint performance and increase the contributions of these two functions. Among their findings:

- The marketing function takes different forms in different companies at different product life cycle stages. Marketing's increasing influence in each phase of an organization's growth profoundly affects its relationship with Sales.

- The strains between Sales and Marketing fall into two main categories: economic (a single budget is typically divided between Sales and Marketing, and not always evenly) and cultural (the two functions attract very different types of people who achieve success by spending their time in very different ways).

In this article, the authors describe the four types of relationships Sales and Marketing typically exhibit. They provide a diagnostic to help readers assess their companies' level of integration, and they offer recommendations for more closely aligning the two functions.

Different Roles for Marketing

Before we look closely at the relationship between the two groups, we need to recognize that the nature of the marketing function varies significantly from company to company.

Most small businesses (and most businesses *are* small) don't establish a formal marketing group at all. Their marketing ideas come from managers, the sales force, or an advertising agency. Such businesses equate marketing with selling; they don't conceive of marketing as a broader way to position their firms.

Eventually, successful small businesses add a marketing person (or persons) to help relieve the sales force of some chores. These new staff members conduct research to calibrate the size of the market, choose the best markets and channels, and determine potential buyers' motives and influences. They work with outside agencies on advertising and promotions. They develop collateral materials to help the sales force attract customers and close sales. And, finally, they use direct mail, telemarketing, and trade shows to find and qualify leads for the sales force. Both Sales and Marketing see the marketing group as an adjunct to the sales force at this stage, and the relationship between the functions is usually positive.

As companies become larger and more successful, executives recognize that there is more to marketing than setting the four P's: product, pricing, place, and promotion. They determine that effective marketing calls for people skilled in segmentation, targeting, and positioning. Once companies hire marketers with those skills, Marketing becomes an independent player. It also starts to compete with Sales for funding. While the sales mission has not changed, the marketing mission has. Disagreements arise. Each function takes on tasks it believes the other should be doing but isn't. All too often, organizations find that they have a marketing function inside Sales, and a sales function inside Marketing. At this stage, the salespeople wish that the marketers would worry about future opportunities (long-term strategy) and leave the current opportunities (individual and group sales) to them.

Once the marketing group tackles higher-level tasks like segmentation, it starts to work more closely with other departments, particularly Strategic Planning, Product Development, Finance, and Manufacturing. The company starts to think in terms of developing brands rather than products, and brand managers become powerful players in the organization. The marketing group is no longer a humble ancillary to the sales department. It sets its sights much higher: The marketers believe it's essential to transform the organization into a "marketingled" company. As they introduce this rhetoric, others in the firm—including the sales group—question whether the marketers have the competencies, experience, and understanding to lead the organization. While Marketing increases its influence within separate business units, it rarely becomes a major force at the corporate level. There are exceptions: Citigroup, Coca-Cola, General Electric, IBM, and Microsoft each have a marketing head at the corporate level. And Marketing is more apt to drive company strategy in major packaged-goods companies such as General Mills, Kraft, and Procter & Gamble. Even then, though, during economic downturns, Marketing is more closely questioned—and its workforce more likely to be cut—than Sales.

Why Can't They Just Get Along?

There are two sources of friction between Sales and Marketing. One is economic, and the other is cultural. The economic friction is generated by the need to divide the total budget granted by senior management to support Sales and Marketing. In fact, the sales force is apt to criticize how Marketing spends money on three of the four P's—pricing, promotion, and product. Take pricing. The marketing group is under pressure to achieve revenue goals and wants the sales force to "sell the price" as opposed to "selling through price." The salespeople usually favor lower prices because they can sell the product more easily and because low prices give them more room to negotiate. In addition, there are organizational tensions around pricing decisions. While Marketing is responsible for setting suggested retail or list prices and establishing promotional pricing, Sales has the final say over transactional pricing. When special low pricing is required, Marketing frequently has no input. The vice president of sales goes directly to the CFO. This does not make the marketing group happy.

Promotion costs, too, are a source of friction. The marketing group needs to spend money to generate customers' awareness of, interest in, preference for, and desire for a product. But the sales force often views the large sums spent on promotion—particularly on television advertising—as a waste of money. The VP of sales tends to think that this money would be better spent increasing the size and quality of the sales force.

When marketers help set the other P, the product being launched, salespeople often complain that it lacks the features, style, or quality their customers want. That's because the sales group's worldview is shaped by the needs of its individual customers. The marketing team, however, is concerned about releasing products whose features have broad appeal.

The budget for both groups also reflects which department wields more power within the organization, a significant factor. CEOs tend to favor the sales group when setting budgets. One chief executive told us, "Why should I invest in more marketing when I can get better results by hiring more salespeople?" CEOs often see sales as more tangible, with more short-run impact. The sales group's contributions to the bottom line are also easier to judge than the marketers' contributions.

The cultural conflict between Sales and Marketing is, if anything, even more entrenched than the economic conflict. This is true in part because the two functions attract different types of people who spend their time in very different ways. Marketers, who until recently had more formal education than salespeople, are highly analytical, data oriented, and project focused. They're all about building competitive advantage for the future. They judge their projects' performance with a cold eye, and they're ruthless with a failed initiative. However, that performance focus doesn't always look like action to their colleagues in Sales because it all happens behind a desk rather than out in the field. Salespeople, in contrast, spend their time talking to existing and potential customers. They're skilled relationship builders; they're not only savvy about customers' willingness to buy but also attuned to which product features will fly and which will die. They want to keep moving. They're used to rejection, and it doesn't depress them. They live for closing a sale. It's hardly surprising that these two groups of people find it difficult to work well together.

If the organization doesn't align incentives carefully, the two groups also run into conflicts about seemingly simple things—for instance, which products to focus on selling. Salespeople may push products with lower margins that satisfy quota goals, while Marketing wants them to sell products with higher profit margins and more promising futures. More broadly speaking, the two groups' performance is judged very differently. Salespeople make a living by closing sales, full stop. It's easy to see who (and what) is successful—almost immediately. But the marketing budget is devoted to programs, not people, and it takes much longer to know whether a program has helped to create long-term competitive advantage for the organization.

Four Types of Relationships

Given the potential economic and cultural conflicts, one would expect some strains to develop between the two groups. And, indeed, some level of dysfunction usually does exist, even in cases where the heads of Sales and Marketing are friendly. The sales and marketing departments in the companies we studied exhibit four types of relationships. The relationships change as the companies' marketing and sales functions mature—the groups move from being unaligned (and often conflicted) to being fully integrated (and usually conflict-free)—though we've seen only a few cases where the two functions are fully integrated.

Undefined
When the relationship is undefined, Sales and Marketing have grown independently; each is preoccupied largely with its own tasks and agendas. Each group doesn't know much about what the other is up to—until a conflict arises. Meetings between the two, which are ad hoc, are likely to be devoted to conflict resolution rather than proactive cooperation.

Defined
In a defined relationship, the two groups set up processes—and rules—to prevent disputes. There's a "good fences make good neighbors" orientation; the marketers and salespeople know who is supposed to do what, and they stick to their own tasks for the most part. The groups start to build a common language in potentially

How well do Sales and Marketing work together?

This instrument is intended to help you gauge how well your sales and marketing groups are aligned and integrated. Ask your heads of Sales and Marketing (as well as their staffs) to evaluate each of the following statements on a scale of 1 to 5, where 1 is "strongly disagree" and 5 is "strongly agree." Tally the numbers, and use the scoring key to determine the kind of relationship Sales and Marketing have in your company. The higher the score, the more integrated the relationship. (Several companies have found that their sales forces and their marketing staffs have significantly different perceptions about how well they work together—which in itself is quite interesting.)

Scoring

20–39 Undefined	60–79 Aligned
40–59 Defined	80–100 Integrated

	Strongly disagree	Disagree	Neither	Agree	Strongly agree
	1	2	3	4	5
1. Our sales figures are usually close to the sales forecast.					
2. If things go wrong, or results are disappointing, neither function points fingers or blames the other.					
3. Marketing people often meet with key customers during the sales process.					
4. Marketing solicits participation from Sales in drafting the marketing plan.					

5. Our salespeople believe the collateral supplied by Marketing is a valuable tool to help them get more sales.

6. The sales force willingly cooperates in supplying feedback requested by Marketing.

7. There is a great deal of common language here between Sales and Marketing.

8. The heads of Sales and Marketing regularly confer about upstream issues such as idea generation, market sensing, and product development strategy.

9. Sales and Marketing work closely together to define segment buying behavior.

10. When Sales and Marketing meet, they do not need to spend much time on dispute resolution and crisis management.

11. The heads of Sales and Marketing work together on business planning for products and services that will not be launched for two or more years.

12. We discuss and use common metrics for determining the success of Sales and Marketing.

13. Marketing actively participates in defining and executing the sales strategy for individual key accounts.

14. Sales and Marketing manage their activities using jointly developed business funnels, processes, or pipelines that span the business chain—from initial market sensing to customer service.

15. Marketing makes a significant contribution to analyzing data from the sales funnel and using those data to improve the predictability and effectiveness of the funnel.

(continued)

	Strongly disagree 1	Disagree 2	Neither 3	Agree 4	Strongly agree 5
16. Sales and Marketing share a strong "We rise or fall together" culture.	——	——	——	——	——
17. Sales and Marketing report to a single chief customer officer, chief revenue officer, or equivalent C-level executive.	——	——	——	——	——
18. There's significant interchange of people between Sales and Marketing.	——	——	——	——	——
19. Sales and Marketing jointly develop and deploy training programs, events, and learning opportunities for their respective staffs.	——	——	——	——	——
20. Sales and Marketing actively participate in the preparation and presentation of each other's plans to top executives.	——	——	——	——	——

____ + ____ + ____ + ____ + ____ = ____ Total contentious areas, such as "How do we define a lead?" Meetings become more reflective; people raise questions like "What do we expect of one another?" The groups work together on large events like customer conferences and trade shows.

Aligned

When Sales and Marketing are aligned, clear boundaries between the two exist, but they're flexible. The groups engage in joint planning and training. The sales group understands and uses marketing terminology such as "value proposition" and "brand image." Marketers confer with salespeople on important accounts. They play a role in transactional, or commodity, sales as well.

Integrated

When Sales and Marketing are fully integrated, boundaries become blurred. Both groups redesign the relationship to share structures, systems, and rewards. Marketing—and to a lesser degree Sales—begins to focus on strategic, forward-thinking types of tasks (market sensing, for instance) and sometimes splits into upstream and downstream groups. Marketers are deeply embedded in the management of key accounts. The two groups develop and implement shared metrics. Budgeting becomes more flexible and less contentious. A "rise or fall together" culture develops.

We designed an assessment tool that can help organizations gauge the relationship between their sales and marketing departments. (See the exhibit "How well do Sales and Marketing work together?") We originally developed this instrument to help us understand what we were seeing in our research, but the executives we were studying quickly appropriated it for their own use. Without an objective tool of this kind, it's very difficult for managers to judge their cultures and their working environments.

Moving Up

Once an organization understands the nature of the relationship between its marketing and sales groups, senior managers may wish to create a stronger alignment between the two. (It's not always necessary, however. The sidebar "Do We Need to Be More Aligned?" can help organizations decide whether to make a change.)

Moving from undefined to defined

If the business unit or company is small, members of Sales and Marketing may enjoy good, informal relationships that needn't be disturbed. This is especially true if Marketing's role is primarily to support the sales force. However, senior managers should intervene if conflicts arise regularly. As we noted earlier, this generally happens because the groups are competing for scarce resources and because their respective roles haven't been clearly defined. At this stage, managers need to create clear rules of engagement, including handoff points for important tasks like following up on sales leads.

Moving from defined to aligned

The defined state can be comfortable for both parties. "It may not be perfect," one VP of sales told us, "but it's a whole lot better than it was." Staying at this level won't work, though, if your industry is changing in significant ways. If the market is becoming commoditized, for example, a traditional sales force may become costly. Or if the market is moving toward customization, the sales force will need to upgrade its skills. The heads of Sales and Marketing may want to build a more aligned relationship and jointly add new skills. To move from a defined relationship to an aligned one:

Encourage disciplined communication. When it comes to improving relations between any two functions, the first step inevitably involves improving communication. But it's not as simple as just *increasing* communication between two groups. More communication is expensive. It eats up time, and it prolongs decision making. We advocate instead for more *disciplined* communication. Hold regular meetings between Sales and Marketing (at least quarterly, perhaps bimonthly or monthly). Make sure that major opportunities, as well as any problems, are on the agenda. Focus the discussions on action items that will resolve problems, and perhaps even create opportunities, by the next meeting. Salespeople and marketers need to know

Do We Need to Be More Aligned?

THE NATURE OF RELATIONS BETWEEN Sales and Marketing in your organization can run the gamut—from undefined (the groups act independent of one another) to integrated (the groups share structures, systems, and rewards). Not every company will want to—or should—move from being undefined to being defined or from being defined to being aligned. The following exhibit can help you decide under which circumstances your company should more tightly integrate its sales and marketing functions.

	Undefined	Defined	Aligned
Don't make any changes if...	The company is small. The company has good informal relationships. Marketing is still a sales support function.	The company's products and services are fairly cut-and-dried. Traditional marketing and sales roles work in this market. There's no clear and compelling reason to change.	The company lacks a culture of shared responsibility. Sales and Marketing report separately. The sales cycle is fairly short.
Tighten the relationship between Sales and Marketing if...	Conflicts are evident between the two functions. There's duplication of effort between the functions; or tasks are falling through the cracks. The functions compete for resources or funding.	Even with careful definition of roles, there's duplication of effort between the functions; or tasks are falling through the cracks. The market is commoditized and makes a traditional sales force costly. Products are developed, prototyped, or extensively customized during the sales process. Product life cycles are shortening, and technology turnover is accelerating.	A common process or business funnel can be created for managing and measuring revenue-generating activities.
	Move to defined ▷	Move to aligned ▷	Move to integrated ▷

when and *with whom* they should communicate. Companies should develop systematic processes and guidelines such as, "You should involve the brand manager whenever the sales opportunity is above $2 million," or "We will not go to print on any marketing collateral until salespeople have reviewed it," or "Marketing will be invited to the top ten critical account reviews." Businesses also need to establish an up-to-date, user-friendly "who to call" database. People get frustrated—and they waste time—searching in the wrong places for help.

Create joint assignments; rotate jobs. As your functions become better aligned, it's important to create opportunities for marketers and salespeople to work together. This will make them more familiar with each other's ways of thinking and acting. It's useful for marketers, particularly brand managers and researchers, to occasionally go along on sales calls. They should get involved with developing alternate solutions for customers, early in the sales process. And they should also sit in on important account-planning sessions. Salespeople, in turn, should help to develop marketing plans and should sit in on product-planning reviews. They should preview ad and sales-promotion campaigns. They should share their deep knowledge about customers' purchasing habits. Jointly, marketers and salespeople should generate a playbook for expanding business with the top ten accounts in each market segment. They should also plan events and conferences together.

Appoint a liaison from Marketing to work with the sales force. The liaison needs to be someone both groups trust. He or she helps to resolve conflicts and shares with each group the tacit knowledge from the other group. It's important not to micromanage the liaison's activities. One of the Marketing respondents in our study described the liaison's role this way: "This is a person who lives with the sales force. He goes to the staff meetings, he goes to the client meetings, and he goes to the client strategy meetings. He doesn't develop product; he comes back and says, 'Here's what this market needs. Here's what's emerging,' and then he works hand in hand with the salesperson and the key customer to develop products."

Colocate marketers and salespeople. It's an old and simple truth that when people are physically close, they will interact more often and are more likely to work well together. One bank we studied located its sales and marketing functions in an empty shopping mall: Different groups and teams within Sales and Marketing were each allocated a storefront. Particularly in the early stages of moving functions toward a more closely aligned relationship, this kind of proximity is a big advantage. Most companies, though, centralize their marketing function, while the members of their sales group remain geographically dispersed. Such organizations need to work harder to facilitate communication between Sales and Marketing and to create shared work.

Improve sales force feedback. Marketers commonly complain that salespeople are too busy to share their experiences, ideas, and insights. Indeed, very few salespeople have an incentive to spend their precious time sharing customer information with Marketing. They have quotas to reach, after all, and limited time in which to meet and sell to customers. To more closely align Sales and Marketing, senior managers need to ensure that the sales force's experience can be tapped with a minimum of disruption. For instance, Marketing can ask the Sales VP to summarize any sales force insights for the month or the quarter. Or Marketing can design shorter information forms, review call reports and CRM data independently, or pay salespeople to make themselves available to interviewers from the marketing group and to summarize what their sales colleagues are thinking about.

Moving from aligned to integrated

Most organizations will function well when Sales and Marketing are aligned. This is especially true if the sales cycle is relatively short, the sales process is fairly straightforward, and the company doesn't have a strong culture of shared responsibility. In complicated or quickly changing situations, there are good reasons to move Sales and Marketing into an integrated relationship. (The exhibit "Sales and Marketing integration checklist" outlines the issues you'll want

Sales and Marketing integration checklist

To achieve integration between Sales and Marketing, your company needs to focus on the following tasks.

Integrate activities	Integrate processes and systems	Enable the culture	Integrate organizational structures
☐ Jointly involve Sales and Marketing in product planning and in setting sales targets.	☐ Implement systems to track and manage Sales and Marketing's joint activities.	☐ Emphasize shared responsibility for results between the different divisions of the organization.	☐ Split Marketing into upstream and downstream teams.
☐ Jointly involve Sales and Marketing in generating value propositions for different market segments.	☐ Utilize and regularly update shared databases.	☐ Emphasize metrics.	☐ Hire a chief revenue officer.
☐ Jointly involve Sales and Marketing in assessing customer needs.	☐ Establish common metrics for evaluating the overall success of Sales and Marketing efforts.	☐ Tie rewards to results.	
☐ Jointly involve Sales and Marketing in signing off on advertising materials.	☐ Create reward systems to laud successful efforts by Sales and Marketing.	☐ Enforce divisions' conformity to systems and processes.	
☐ Jointly involve Sales and Marketing in analyzing the top opportunities by segment.	☐ Mandate that teams from Sales and Marketing meet periodically to review and improve relations.		
	☐ Require Sales and Marketing heads to attend each other's budget reviews with the CEO.		

to think through.) This means integrating such straightforward activities as planning, target setting, customer assessment, and value-proposition development. It's tougher, though, to integrate the two groups' processes and systems; these must be replaced with common processes, metrics, and reward systems. Organizations need to develop shared databases, as well as mechanisms for continuous improvement. Hardest of all is changing the culture to support integration. The best examples of integration we found were in companies that already emphasized shared responsibility and disciplined planning; that were metrics driven; that tied rewards to results; and that were managed through systems and processes. To move from an aligned relationship to an integrated one:

Appoint a chief revenue (or customer) officer. The main rationale for integrating Sales and Marketing is that the two functions have a common goal: the generation of profitable and increasing revenue. It is logical to put both functions under one C-level executive. Companies such as Campbell's Soup, Coca-Cola, and FedEx have a chief revenue officer (CRO) who is responsible for planning for and delivering the revenue needed to meet corporate objectives. The CRO needs control over the forces affecting revenue—specifically, marketing, sales, service, and pricing. This manager could also be called the chief customer officer (CCO), a title used in such companies as Kellogg; Sears, Roebuck; and United Air Lines. The CCO may be more of a customer ombudsman or customer advocate in some companies; but the title can also signal an executive's broader responsibility for revenue management.

Define the steps in the marketing and sales funnels. Sales and Marketing are responsible for a sequence of activities and events (sometimes called a funnel) that leads customers toward purchases and, hopefully, ongoing relationships. Such funnels can be described from the customer's perspective or from the seller's perspective. (A typical funnel based on the customer's decision sequence is shown in the sidebar "The Buying Funnel.") Marketing is usually responsible for the first few steps—building customers'

The Buying Funnel

THERE'S A CONVENTIONAL VIEW that Marketing should take responsibility for the first four steps of the typical buying funnel—customer awareness, brand awareness, brand consideration, and brand preference. (The funnel reflects the ways that Marketing and Sales influence customers' purchasing decisions.) Marketing builds brand preference, creates a marketing plan, and generates leads for sales before handing off execution and follow-up tasks to Sales. This division of labor keeps Marketing focused on strategic activities and prevents the group from intruding in individual sales opportunities. But if things do not go well, the blame game begins. Sales criticizes the plan for the brand, and Marketing accuses Sales of not working hard enough or smart enough.

The sales group is responsible for the last four steps of the funnel—purchase intention, purchase, customer loyalty, and customer advocacy. Sales usually develops its own funnel for the selling tasks that happen during the first two steps. (These include prospecting, defining needs, preparing and presenting proposals, negotiating contracts, and implementing the sale.) Apart from some lead generation in the prospecting stage, Marketing all too often plays no role in these tasks.

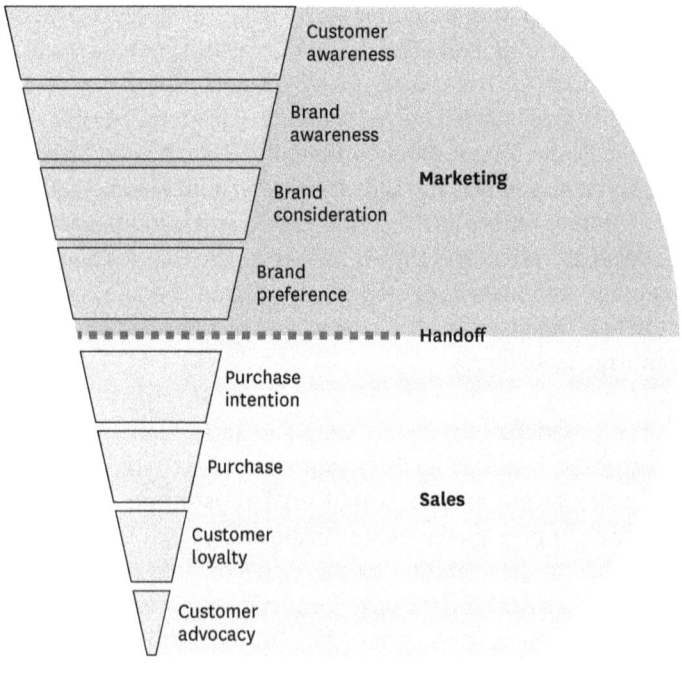

brand awareness and brand preference, creating a marketing plan, and generating leads for sales. Then Sales executes the marketing plan and follows up on leads. This division of labor has merit. It is simple, and it prevents Marketing from getting too involved in individual sales opportunities at the expense of more strategic activities. But the handoff brings serious penalties. If things do not go well, Sales can say that the plan was weak, and Marketing can say that the salespeople did not work hard enough or smart enough. And in companies where Marketing makes a handoff, marketers can lose touch with active customers. Meanwhile, Sales usually develops its own funnel describing the sequence of selling tasks. Funnels of this kind—integrated into the CRM system and into sales forecasting and account-review processes—form an increasingly important backbone for sales management. Unfortunately, Marketing often plays no role in these processes. Some companies in our study, however, have integrated Marketing into the sales funnel. During prospecting and qualifying, for instance, Marketing helps Sales to create common standards for leads and opportunities. During the needs-definition stage, Marketing helps Sales develop value propositions. In the solution-development phase, Marketing provides "solution collateral"—organized templates and customizing guides so salespeople can develop solutions for customers without constantly having to reinvent the wheel. When customers are nearing a decision, Marketing contributes case study material, success stories, and site visits to help address customers' concerns. And during contract negotiations, Marketing advises the sales team on planning and pricing. Of course, Marketing's involvement in the sales funnel should be matched by Sales' involvement in the upstream, strategic decisions the marketing group is making. Salespeople should work with the marketing and R&D staffs as they decide how to segment the market, which products to offer to which segments, and how to position those products.

Split Marketing into two groups. There's a strong case for splitting Marketing into upstream (strategic) and downstream (tactical) groups. Downstream marketers develop advertising and promotion campaigns, collateral material, case histories, and sales tools. They help salespeople develop and qualify leads. The downstream team uses market research and feedback from the sales reps to help sell existing products in new market segments, to create new messages, and to design better sales tools. Upstream marketers engage in customer sensing. That is, they monitor the voice of the customer and develop a long view of the company's business opportunities and threats. The upstream team shares its insights with senior managers and product developers—and it participates in product development.

Set shared revenue targets and reward systems. The integrated organization will not succeed unless Sales and Marketing share responsibility for revenue objectives. One marketing manager told us, "I'm going to use whatever tools I need to make sure Sales is effective, because, at the end of the day, I'm judged on that sales target as well." One of the barriers to shared objectives, however, is the thorny issue of shared rewards. Salespeople historically work on commission, and marketers don't. To successfully integrate the two functions, management will need to review the overall compensation policy.

Integrate Sales and Marketing metrics. The need for common metrics becomes critical as Marketing becomes more embedded in the sales process and as Sales plays a more active role in Marketing. "In order to be the customer-intimate company we are," says Larry Norman, president of Financial Markets Group, part of the Aegon USA operating companies, "we need to be metrics driven and have metrics in place that track both sales and marketing performance." On a macro level, companies like General Electric have "the number"—the sales goal to which both Sales and Marketing commit. There is no escaping the fact that, however well integrated Sales and Marketing are, the company will also want to develop metrics to measure and reward each group appropriately.

Sales metrics are easier to define and track. Some of the most common measures are percent of sales quota achieved, number of new customers, number of sales closings, average gross profit per customer, and sales expense to total sales. When downstream marketers become embedded in the sales process—for example, as members of critical account teams—it's only logical to measure and reward their performance using sales metrics. But then how should the company evaluate its upstream marketers? On the basis of the accuracy of their product forecasting, or the number of new market segments they discover? The metrics will vary according to the type of marketing job. Senior managers need to establish different measures for brand managers, market researchers, marketing information systems managers, advertising managers, sales promotion managers, market segment managers, and product managers. It's easier to construct a set of metrics if the marketers' purposes and tasks are clearly outlined. Still, given that upstream marketers are more engaged in sowing the seeds for a better future than in helping to reap the current harvest, the metrics used to judge their performance necessarily become softer and more judgmental.

Obviously, the difference between judging current and future outcomes makes it more complicated for companies to develop common metrics for Sales and Marketing. Upstream marketers in particular need to be assessed according to what they deliver over a longer period. Salespeople, meanwhile, are in the business of converting potential demand into today's sales. As the working relationship between Sales and Marketing becomes more interactive and interdependent, the integrated organization will continue to wrestle with this difficult, but surely not insurmountable, problem.

Senior managers often describe the working relationship between Sales and Marketing as unsatisfactory. The two functions, they say, undercommunicate, underperform, and overcomplain. Not every company will want to—or should—upgrade from defined to aligned relationships or from aligned to integrated relationships. But every company can and should improve the relationship between Sales and Marketing. Carefully planned enhancements will bring salespeople's intimate knowledge of your customers into the company's core. These improvements will also help you serve customers better now and will help you build better products for the future. They will help your company marry softer, relationship-building skills with harder, analytic skills. They will force your organization to closely consider how it rewards people and whether those reward systems apply fairly across functions. Best of all, these improvements will boost both your top-line and bottom-line growth.

Originally published July–August 2006. Reprint R0607E

Match Your Sales Force Structure to Your Business Life Cycle

by Andris A. Zoltners, Prabhakant Sinha, and Sally E. Lorimer

SMART BICYCLE-RACING TEAMS MATCH their strategies to the stages of a race in order to win. In the flat stretches, team members take turns riding in front because it's easier for the team leader to pedal when someone ahead is cutting the wind. In the mountains, some riders make the task easier for the leader by setting the pace and by choosing the best line of ascent. In the time trials, a few team members maintain steady speeds over long distances to lower the team's average finishing time. Talent always matters, but in most races, the way teams deploy talent over time, in different formations in different contexts, makes the difference between winning and losing.

That's a lesson sales leaders must learn. Although companies devote considerable time and money to managing their sales forces, few focus much thought on how the sales force needs to change over the life cycle of a product or a business. However, shifts in the sales force's structure are essential if a company wants to keep winning the race for customers. Specifically, companies must alter four factors over time: the roles that the sales force and selling partners play; the size of the sales force; the sales force's degree of specialization; and how salespeople apportion their efforts among different customers, products, and activities. These variables are critical because they determine how quickly sales forces respond to market opportunities; they influence sales forces' performance; and they affect companies' revenues, costs, and profitability.

Admittedly, it isn't easy for a company to change the composition and activities of its sales force. Salespeople and customers resist change, often quite fiercely. If a company starts hiring specialists instead of general-purpose salespeople, for example, or reassigns accounts from sales reps in the field to telesales staff, existing salespeople will have to learn how to sell different products and will have to terminate some customer relationships. If they earn commissions or bonuses, their income may fall in the short run. Customers, too, will have to adjust to new processes and establish relationships with new salespeople. As a result, businesses tend to change their sales structures only when major events—such as the failure to meet targets, a change in rivals' strategies, or mergers—force them to do so.

This conservatism doesn't serve companies well. The sales force structure that works during start-up is different from what works when the business is growing, during its maturity, and through its decline. The four life-cycle phases aren't mutually exclusive; some companies display characteristics of more than one stage at the same time. Many businesses go through the four stages in turn, but when new technologies or markets emerge, companies can also move nonsequentially through the life cycle stages. These days, businesses tend to go through the four phases more quickly than they used to, which makes it even more important to have a flexible sales force.

Over the past 25 years, we and our colleagues at ZS Associates have studied the sales force structures of approximately 2,500 businesses in 68 countries. Our research shows that companies that change their sales force structures in ways that correspond loosely to the stages a product or business goes through in its life cycle are more successful than those that don't.

During start-up, smart companies focus on whether they should depend on selling partners or create their own sales forces. If they decide to set up sales organizations, they pay a lot of attention to sizing them correctly. As companies grow, sizing issues become even more

Idea in Brief

Although companies devote considerable time and money to managing their sales forces, few focus much thought on how the structure of the sales force needs to change over the life cycle of a product or a business. However, the organization and goals of a sales operation have to evolve as businesses start up, grow, mature, and decline if a company wants to keep winning the race for customers.

Specifically, firms must consider and alter four factors over time: the differing roles that internal salespeople and external selling partners should play, the size of the sales force, its degree of specialization, and how salespeople apportion their efforts among different customers, products, and activities. These variables are critical because they determine how quickly sales forces respond to market opportunities, they influence sales reps' performance, and they affect companies' revenues, costs, and profitability.

In this article, the authors use time-series data and cases to explain how, at each stage, firms can best tackle the relevant issues and get the most out of their sales forces. During start-up, smart companies focus on how big their sales staff should be and on whether they can depend upon selling partners. In the growth phase, they concentrate on getting the sales force's degree of specialization and size right. When businesses hit maturity, companies should better allocate existing resources and hire more general-purpose salespeople. Finally, as organizations go into decline, wise sales leaders reduce sales force size and use partners to keep the business afloat for as long as possible.

---

important. In addition, executives must decide when to invest in specialist sales forces. When businesses hit maturity, the emphasis shifts to making sales forces more effective by appointing account managers and better allocating salespeople's resources, and making them more cost-efficient by using less expensive people such as telesales staff and sales assistants. Finally, as organizations go into decline, sales leaders' attention shifts to reducing the size of sales forces and using even more cost-efficient ways to cover markets. In the following pages, we'll explore in depth how companies can develop the best sales force structures for each of the four stages of the business life cycle. (See the exhibit "The four factors for a successful sales force.")

The four factors for a successful sales force

A company must focus on different aspects of its sales force structure over the life cycle of the business, just as it matches customer strategy to the life cycle of a product.

	BUSINESS LIFE CYCLE STAGE			
	Start-up	Growth	Maturity	Decline
	EMPHASIS			
Role of sales force and selling partners	H H H H	H H	H	H H H
Size of sales force	H H H	H H H H	H H	H H H H
Degree of specialization	H	H H H H	H H H	H H
Sales force resource allocation	H H	H	H H H H	H
	UNDERLYING CUSTOMER STRATEGY			
	Create awareness and generate quick product uptake	Penetrate deeper into existing segments and develop new ones	Focus on efficiently serving and retaining existing customers	Emphasize efficiency, protect critical customer relationships, exit unprofitable segments

Start-Up: Making the Right Moves Early

Sales leaders of new companies and new divisions of existing companies are eager to exploit opportunities in the marketplace and are under pressure to demonstrate success quickly. While a start-up has to worry constantly about selling costs, a new division can draw on some of the parent company's financial and human resources. Still, since both their sales forces must create awareness about new products and generate quick sales, the organizations face the same structural dilemmas.

Do it yourself, or outsource?
The central decision that a new business must make is whether it should sell its products directly to customers or sell them through partners. Although many entrepreneurs outsource the sales function, that may not always be the right decision.

To be sure, by tying up with other companies, new ventures save the costs of building and maintaining sales forces. Partnerships can also help executives manage risk better since start-ups often pay only commissions on sales; if products don't sell, their costs are minimal. Moreover, new businesses can enter markets rapidly by working alongside companies that have sales expertise, influence over sales channels, and relationships with potential customers. For example, in the 1990s, Siebel Systems used systems integration consultants, such as Accenture, to build its enterprise software business quickly.

Companies that decide to outsource the sales function should segment the market and develop sales processes that meet each segment's needs. Then they should select a partner, or partners, that will implement those selling processes effectively. To succeed, a company needs its selling partners' attention. Start-ups must develop partner management systems that include marketing programs and incentive schemes and appoint partner managers who provide selling partners with encouragement, process assistance, sales analytics, and end-user data. All too frequently, companies rely on money to motivate partners, not realizing that incentives aren't a substitute for systems and supervision. Companies should track performance closely, quickly terminate agreements with partners that don't perform well, and shift to selling directly when it's in their long-term interest to do so.

In our experience, many businesses depend on their selling partners for too long. When companies outsource the sales function, they don't control the selling activity, have little power over salespeople, gain no channel power, and don't own customer relationships. As time goes by, it becomes more, not less, difficult to reduce dependence on selling partners. Many firms become stuck in partnerships that inhibit growth. Take the case of SonoSite. When it launched the world's first handheld ultrasound machine in 1999, the company decided to use a well-known distributor to sell the product in the United States. Since the ultrasound device was technologically complex, the distributor needed to educate potential customers. That required a multistep selling process, which the distributor didn't use for the other products it sold. After two years of disappointing sales, SonoSite dropped the distributor and started selling the device itself. A year after it had staffed its sales force fully, its revenues rose by 79%.

Although outsourcing is popular today, we're convinced that companies should use selling partners only if they stand to gain strategic advantages as well as cost benefits. Those advantages come in several flavors. Many partners turn products into solutions, which can greatly increase sales. For example, value-added resellers create systems that combine their own software with computer hardware from different manufacturers. Start-ups also gain access to customers when their products become part of an assortment that a partner offers. For instance, a computer accessories manufacturer could benefit by tying up with distributor CDW, which delivers a range of computer-related equipment to companies in the United States. Only when partners provide strategic advantages are selling relationships likely to endure.

How big should the sales staff be?

During the start-up phase, sales forces have to educate potential customers about products and change customers' buying processes before they can generate sales. Salespeople also must chase down and make every possible sale in order to drive business. That's a lot of work, but new ventures have limited capital to invest in attracting and developing good salespeople. As a result, many new businesses adopt an "earn your way" approach to sizing their sales forces—they start small and add more feet on the street after they have generated the money to pay for them.

This approach sounds eminently logical but often results in companies leaving money on the table (see the exhibit "How sales sizing strategies stack up"). Between 1998 and 2004, we forecast the sales and profit implications of different sales force sizes for 11 start-ups in the health care industry. In ten of the companies, sales leaders chose to create teams that were smaller than the optimal size. In fact, the average size was just 64% of the optimal. By not hiring enough salespeople, each of those companies missed the opportunity to earn tens of millions of dollars in additional sales and profits in their first three years. Tellingly, only one business sized its sales force optimally during the start-up stage—and it went on to become the leader in an overcrowded market segment.

How sales sizing strategies stack up

In their infancy, companies often undersize sales forces. The charts show the impact of three different sizing scenarios on one pharmaceutical company's profits. The figures are projections based on mathematical models. The pharmaceutical company, which started with 300 salespeople, found that an "earn your way" approach to staffing (increasing the sales force only as fast as revenues increase) resulted in the highest first-year contribution, but it yielded the lowest three-year contribution. The longer-term contribution was highest with a "quick build" strategy (quickly ramping up the size of the sales force to the long-term optimal level).

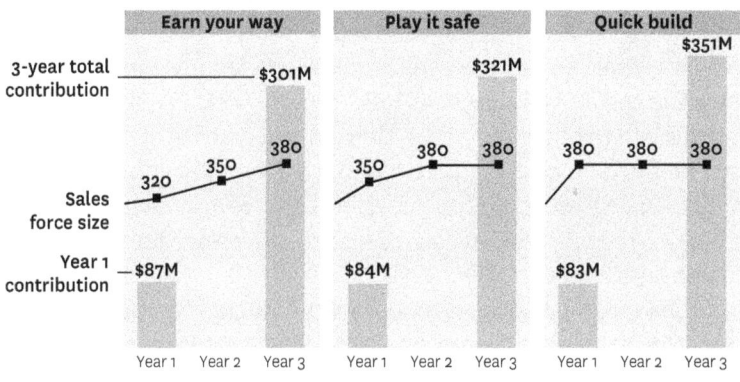

We don't fault sales leaders for investing cautiously when they are short of cash or if the future is uncertain. The trouble is, most companies don't increase their investments in sales forces even when the future becomes clear. The moment signs of success emerge, businesses should increase the size of their sales forces quickly and aggressively. Otherwise, they will forfeit sales and profits—and, perhaps, even their futures.

On the flip side, start-up divisions of existing companies often overinvest in salespeople. Their desire to be competitive results in sales forces that, given the nature of the business opportunity, are too big to be profitable.

Growth: Building on Success

During the start-up stage, many companies' product lines are narrow, and they operate in a small number of markets. As businesses grow, their product portfolios expand, and their sales forces have to call on prospects in a broader set of markets. This presents sales managers with two challenges: specialization and size.

The need to specialize

In the growth phase, it's not sufficient for many companies to maintain a sales force of generalists who sell the entire product line to all markets. Salespeople need to master multiple products, markets, and selling tasks at this stage. As repeat sales become a larger proportion of sales, customers will require service and support, adding to salespeople's workloads. As tasks grow beyond the salespeople's capacity to perform their jobs, they are likely to drop the customers, products, and selling activities that are most difficult to manage. Unfortunately, what they drop may be lucrative or strategic opportunities for the business. At this point, companies need to set up specialist sales forces.

Some specialist sales teams focus on products, others on markets, and still others on customer segments. Sales forces can also specialize in certain activities: Some salespeople concentrate on acquiring customers and others on servicing existing customers. Every kind of specialization has benefits and costs. For instance, specialization by markets reduces salespeople's focus on products, while product or activity specialization forces customers to deal with multiple salespeople. Many companies therefore create hybrid structures that include a mix of generalists as well as market, product, and activity specialists. One well-known software company has hired account managers to focus on all the needs of its major customers. The company's product specialists call on midsize clients that don't generate enough business to warrant account managers, and its generalist salespeople cover small companies whose needs don't justify visits by several product specialists.

The transition from a multipurpose sales force to a specialized one is always tough. The work changes considerably, and customer relationships are disrupted. Sales forces may need to adopt team-based selling techniques, making coordination and collaboration vital. The people who succeed in a team-based setting are likely to be different from the lone wolves who do well in a traditional sales force. Consequently, companies may have to recast parts of their sales forces.

Rejuvenated businesses face a slightly different predicament. When a company goes back into growth gear after a period of maturity or decline, its new offerings will have different value propositions and will open up new markets. Salespeople will need to sell differently, and they'll need retraining to do so. Companies may consider splitting their sales forces into groups that specialize in selling old and new products. If neither education nor restructuring delivers results, the company may have to replace the sales force.

Companies must revisit sizing issues when they move from generalist sales forces to specialist ones. On the one hand, specialists will have to cover larger distances than generalists did in order to call on the same number of customers; this means they'll lose time in travel. The company will therefore need more of them to cover its customer base. On the other hand, specialists are more effective than generalists are, so each sales call will be more profitable.

Getting the size right

Growth is usually a happy time in the evolution of a sales force. Sales come in relatively easily, and salespeople are full of optimism. Even so, companies often make critical errors in sizing their sales forces. They continue to understaff, and as a result, they're unable to capitalize on all the opportunities that exist.

Most companies invest conservatively in salespeople because they don't realize that increasing the size of the sales force has short-term and long-term consequences. When new salespeople come on board, they initially generate small revenue increases. As time goes by, their impact gets bigger. That happens for several reasons. First, new salespeople are not as effective as they will be when they become veterans. Second, in markets with long selling cycles, it takes months of effort before salespeople clinch sales. Third, many purchases, especially in business markets, are not onetime orders but multiyear contracts. Finally, carryover sales—sales that accrue in the future but are the result of sales efforts in the present—vary across products and markets, but they represent a significant portion of every company's long-term revenues.

When a company increases the size of its sales force, it doesn't maximize sales or profits at first. Over time, however, the company will make more profits than if it had started with a smaller sales force. We analyzed data from sizing studies that ZS Associates conducted between 1998 and 2001 for 50 companies. We found that the sales force size that maximizes companies' three-year profits is 18% larger, on average, than the size that maximizes one-year profits. Such findings create competing priorities for sales leaders, who want long-term success but feel pressure to meet annual profit targets. Besides, they rightly believe that three-year projections are less accurate than one-year forecasts. A cautious approach is justified if there is considerable uncertainty over the future, but most sales leaders favor cost-minimizing tactics over profit-maximizing ones, even when the likelihood of success is high. Consequently, they don't hire enough salespeople to exploit the market fully.

Behavioral influences, too, exert pressure on executives to keep sales forces small. Most salespeople resist giving up accounts. They argue that new sales territories aren't justified; some threaten to join competitors if management reduces their accounts bases. For instance, in 2005, when an American medical devices company set out to add 25 sales territories, salespeople and sales managers resisted. They exerted so much pressure that the company eventually created only 12 new territories, which resulted in lower sales and profits than the business could have generated by hiring more salespeople.

Sales leaders can reduce this kind of resistance by fostering a culture of change. They must set expectations early, so that salespeople realize from the outset that, as the business grows, there will be changes in territories and compensation. Some companies periodically reassign accounts between territories to maintain the right balance. Others set lower commission rates on repeat sales, or pay commissions, after the first year, only after a salesperson's revenues exceed a certain level. These tactics give companies the flexibility to expand territories and sales forces in the future.

A company should determine the most appropriate size for its sales force by evaluating the probable size of the opportunity and assessing the potential risks of pursuing an aggressive or conservative approach. An aggressive strategy is appropriate when the business has a high likelihood of success and management has confidence in the sales projections. A more conservative strategy works when greater uncertainty surrounds the business's success.

Two types of sizing errors are common. First, if sales force growth is aggressive, but the market opportunity is moderate, the company will end up having to reduce its sales force. Second, if sales force growth is conservative, but the market opportunity is large, a business may forfeit its best chance to become a market leader. To make better decisions about sales force sizing, companies must invest in market research and in developing forecasting methods and sales response analytics. (See the sidebar "Sizing the Sales Force by the Numbers.")

Sizing the Sales Force by the Numbers

EVERY COMPANY IN GROWTH MODE should conduct a break-even analysis to check if its sales force is the right size. That involves computing the break-even ratio (the ratio of the incremental sales revenue per additional salesperson to the break-even sales), estimating the carryover sales rates, and using those estimates to determine the three-year return on investment in sales staff.

To determine the break-even ratio:

1. Estimate the annual cost of a salesperson (**C**), the gross margin (**M**), which is the amount of sales revenue that the business keeps as profit after deducting variable costs, and the gross margin rate (M_R), which is gross margin expressed as a percentage of sales revenue.

2. Calculate break-even sales by dividing the cost of a salesperson by the gross margin rate (**C** ÷ M_R = **B**). That's the amount a salesperson must sell in a year to cover his or her costs.

3. Estimate the incremental sales revenue that an additional salesperson could generate in a year (**I**).

4. Divide the incremental sales revenue per additional salesperson by the break-even sales to compute the break-even ratio (**I** ÷ **B**). A ratio of 2.00, for instance, implies that a new salesperson will generate gross margin equal to twice his or her cost in a year.

> Break-even =

MATCH YOUR SALES FORCE STRUCTURE TO YOUR BUSINESS LIFE CYCLE

To determine the carryover sales percentage:

5. Estimate the percentage, based on past trends, of this year's sales that the company will retain in future years without any sales force effort. Those are the carryover sales percentages (K_2 for next year and K_3 for the year after).

$$\text{Carryover} = \overline{K_2} \quad \overline{K_3}$$

To determine the three-year ROI on sales staff:

6. Take the sum of the gross margin on the incremental sales revenue that an additional salesperson can generate in year 1, the incremental gross margin on carryover sales in year 2, and the incremental gross margin on carryover sales in year 3.

7. Subtract from that sum the annual cost of an additional salesperson.

8. Divide the total by the additional salesperson's annual cost. The result is expressed as a percentage. The formula looks like this: $[(M_R \times I) + (M_R \times I \times K_2) + (M_R \times I \times K_3) - C] \div C$

$$\text{ROI} =$$

The break-even ratio and the first-year carryover rate can tell you how to size your sales force. In the table below, the numbers in each cell represent three-year returns on sales force investment. Businesses can set their own criteria, but in our experience, companies have sized their sales forces optimally when the ROI is between 50% and 150%. If the ROI is below 50%, the sales force is too large, and if it is over 150%, the force is too small.

(continued)

New salesperson sales/Break-even sales	Carryover									
	0%	10%	20%	30%	40%	50%	60%	70%	80%	90%
0.25	-75%	-72%	-69%	-65%	-61%	-56%	-51%	-45%	-39%	-32%
0.50	-50%	-45%	-38%	-31%	-22%	-13%	-2%	10%	22%	36%
0.75	-25%	-17%	-7%	4%	17%	31%	47%	64%	83%	103%
1.00	0%	11%	24%	39%	56%	75%	96%	119%	144%	171%
1.25	25%	39%	55%	74%	95%	119%	145%	174%	205%	239%
1.50	50%	67%	86%	109%	134%	163%	194%	229%	266%	307%
1.75	75%	94%	117%	143%	173%	206%	243%	283%	327%	374%
2.00	100%	122%	148%	178%	212%	250%	292%	338%	388%	442%
2.25	125%	150%	179%	213%	251%	294%	341%	393%	449%	510%
2.50	150%	178%	210%	248%	290%	338%	390%	448%	510%	578%
2.75	175%	205%	241%	282%	329%	381%	439%	502%	571%	645%
3.00	200%	233%	272%	317%	368%	425%	488%	557%	632%	713%
3.25	225%	261%	303%	352%	407%	469%	537%	612%	693%	781%
3.50	250%	289%	334%	387%	446%	513%	586%	667%	754%	849%
3.75	275%	316%	365%	421%	485%	556%	635%	721%	815%	916%
4.00	300%	344%	396%	456%	524%	600%	684%	776%	876%	984%

☐ Oversized ☐ Right size ▨ Undersized

Maturity: The Quest for Effectiveness and Efficiency

Eventually, products and services start to lose their advantage, competition intensifies, and margins erode. At this stage, sales leaders must rely more on resourcefulness than on increasing the scale of the sales effort. Their strategy should emphasize retaining customers, serving existing segments, and increasing the efficiency and effectiveness of the sales force.

Optimizing resources

In the maturity phase, companies must focus on optimizing the sales force's effectiveness. A study we conducted in 2001 shows that mature companies boosted their gross margins by 4.5% when they resized their sales forces and allocated resources better. While 29% of those gains came because the companies corrected the size of their sales forces, 71% of the gains were the result of changes in resource utilization.

Companies often don't optimize the allocation of their sales resources for several reasons. First, they use the wrong rules. For instance, executives often target customers with the highest potential even though these customers prefer to buy from competitors. Smart companies allocate more resources to products and markets that respond well to salespeople. Second, businesses frequently don't have data on the sales potential of accounts and territories or the responsiveness of potential customers to sales efforts.

There are no shortcuts on the road to effectiveness, though. Organizations can allocate resources best if they measure how responsive different products and markets are to sales efforts. Executives can do that by comparing sales results among similar-sized customers to whom they allotted different levels of effort. That analysis allows a company to evaluate the financial implications of different allocation scenarios. The company can then manage its sales force, even offering incentives on occasion, so that salespeople expend effort in the most productive ways. (See the exhibit "Optimizing the maturity phase.")

Businesses often find sales effort wasted. Some salespeople try to sell everything in the bag; others spend too much time with familiar or easy-to-sell products. Product managers may dangle the

Optimizing the maturity phase

Mature companies optimize their resources when sales forces focus on the customers, products, and selling activities that generate the highest response to their sales efforts. To do that, sales leaders must ask themselves the following questions:

RESOURCE ALLOCATION DECISIONS		
Customer	**Product**	**Activity**
What market segments should we focus on:	What products should we focus on:	What activities should we focus on:
• High volume or low volume?	• Existing or new?	• Hunting for new customers or retaining old customers?
• Highly profitable or less profitable?	• High volume or relatively low volume?	• Selling or servicing?
• National accounts or smaller accounts?	• Easy to sell or hard to sell?	How do we allocate relationship experts, product experts, and industry experts?
• New or old accounts?	• Familiar or unfamiliar?	
What industries do we call on?	• Differentiated or nondifferentiated?	
What geographic areas do we focus on: local, regional, national, or international?	• Products with long selling cycles or short selling cycles?	
Which accounts should headquarters staff call on, and which should field sales call on?	• Products with high short-term impact and low carryover or with low short-term impact and high carryover?	

wrong incentives, distracting salespeople from spending time with more profitable offerings. In mathematical terms, a company maximizes long-term profits from its sales force when the incremental return on sales force effort is equal across products. But according to a study ZS Associates conducted in 2001, the ratio of the largest incremental return to the smallest return often runs as high as 8:1. That suggests a serious misallocation of selling effort among products. For instance, one business we studied wanted 100 salespeople to sell 37 products. Each item would have received, on average, just

2.7% of the sales force's time. An analysis revealed that the company's profits would soar if the sales force concentrated on just eight products. In fact, our studies show that focused strategies usually deliver better results than across-the-board ones. Thus, a company makes the greatest profits when its sales force spends its time with the most valuable subset of customers or with the most valuable products in its basket.

Good territorial alignment—the assignment of accounts, prospects, or geographies to salespeople—is a frequently overlooked productivity tool. When businesses adopt unsystematic approaches to carving up territories, sales force effort will not match customer needs. To measure the extent of the problem, in 2000, we analyzed data from 36 territorial alignment studies that we had conducted in eight industries in the United States and Canada. Our analysis showed that 55% of sales territories were either too large or too small. Because of the mismatches, businesses were passing up between 2% and 7% of revenues every year. Companies can create and maintain territorial alignment by measuring the time and effort necessary to service customers every year. They should take accounts away from salespeople who can't give them sufficient attention and transfer the accounts to those who don't have enough work.

The account manager's emergence
Many a business discovers in the maturity stage that the use of product specialists is posing coordination problems and confusing customers that must deal with several salespeople. Smart companies appoint managers for the largest accounts. These account managers coordinate the sales effort and bring in product specialists when customers need expertise. In addition to increasing revenues, the appointment of account managers boosts customer satisfaction and often reduces selling costs. During an American medical-products company's growth phase in the 1990s, it added a specialist sales force for almost every new product it launched. Eventually, some large hospitals had more than 30 salespeople from the company visiting them every week, many of whom called on the same contacts. Travel costs soared, and, worse, customers became confused by

the large number of salespeople visiting them. Realizing the problem, the company reduced the number of specialist salespeople and added managers to coordinate selling activities at large accounts. That helped the company save costs and strengthen customer relationships.

Companies must also find the most inexpensive ways to get work done. They can use sales assistants and part-time salespeople to woo small or geographically dispersed customers and to sell easy-to-understand products. Businesses can also use telesales staff to perform activities that don't require face-to-face contact with customers. For example, one newspaper company we consulted with hired sales assistants in 2005 to take over several nonselling and administrative tasks. Before the assistants arrived, salespeople spent only 35% of their time with prospects and customers. The assistants' arrival freed them to spend more time on sales-related tasks. In addition, since the assistants received lower salaries than the salespeople did, the sales force's efficiency rose sharply.

Decline: Living to Fight Another Day

Companies go into decline when products lose their edge and customers shift to rivals. As CEOs search for breakout strategies, sales forces must do everything they can to help businesses remain viable. The most vital decisions relate, as they did during the start-up stage, to the sales force's size and the role of selling partners, but executives' choices depend on whether or not they foresee a turnaround.

When a turnaround is likely

Some businesses know their decline is temporary. They plan to boost revenues and profits in the not-too-distant future by launching new products or by merging with other companies. However, turnarounds often demand different sales force structures than the ones companies have. A smart company therefore determines what kind of structure it will need for the sales force to achieve its new goals. Then it identifies and preserves elements of the current structure that are consistent with the one it will need. That's critical; executives shouldn't tear down the parts of the sales organization that will be valuable in the future. For instance, companies often downsize sales forces to save costs in the short run, although they may need more, not fewer, salespeople to implement new strategies.

Many sales leaders take advantage of temporary declines to eliminate mediocrity in their sales forces. Once the turnaround starts, they hire salespeople who are more qualified than the ones they let go. Sometimes what looks like a misallocation of resources is really mediocre performance. Take the case of a Chicago-based software company that was in decline in the 1990s. The company's sales process evolved appropriately, with salespeople becoming skilled at protecting current business. When the firm launched some new products, it realized that few of its salespeople had the skills and appetite to pursue new customers and markets aggressively. Instead of sacking salespeople, the software firm created two roles: current account managers, or "farmers," and new business developers, or "hunters." The veterans continued to manage existing customers, which suited their capabilities, while sales leaders hired most of the new business developers from outside the organization. That helped the software company move quickly from decline to growth.

When a turnaround isn't likely
When further decline is inevitable, sales organizations can only ensure that companies remain profitable for as long as possible. Businesses should use their salespeople to service the most profitable, loyal, and strategically important customers, and service other accounts through low-cost selling resources such as telesales staff or external partners.

Protecting the most loyal customers and the best salespeople are top priorities. Companies need to focus loving attention on key customers that, fearing the salespeople managing their accounts will soon be gone, will entertain competitive offerings. They must reassure these critical accounts about the immediate future, particularly by retaining star salespeople. When the sales force starts to worry about downsizing, the best salespeople will be the first to leave. Even as companies prepare to let other people go, they must pay stars handsomely to keep them. In addition, strong leadership is essential during downsizing, and only timely and straightforward communication from sales leaders can maintain a reasonable level of morale and motivation.

To decide how quickly it should reduce head count, a company must assess the market opportunity that remains and the risks of different downsizing strategies. A gradual sales force reduction works well when the opportunity is declining at a modest rate, but it is a poor strategy when the market is disappearing quickly. Errors are common. Many businesses downsize the sales force slowly, remaining hopeful between each wave of layoffs that the trend will reverse. When it doesn't, the high cost of the sales force will render the company unprofitable faster. One common tactic for gradual downsizing is a hiring freeze. That isn't an effective way to downsize sales forces, particularly when the opportunity decline is significant. Sales force attrition usually doesn't occur quickly, and if salespeople who cover important accounts leave, a hiring freeze will result in suboptimal market coverage.

Rapid sales force reduction is the best course when the market is in a steep decline. Survivors will know they have some kind of job security, customers will have greater confidence about what the future holds, and sales leaders can start building a smaller, more focused sales organization. The risk with rapid sales force reduction, though, is that if the decline turns out to be less severe than expected, more people will lose their jobs than necessary. Although the business will remain profitable for a while, the rate of decline will be greater than if head count reductions had been modest. If there's a lot of uncertainty about the rate at which the market is shrinking, companies should consider downsizing the sales force in small but discrete steps.

Improving the efficiency of sales forces and searching for lower-cost selling channels are critical when companies are in decline. By using less-expensive selling resources, companies can continue selling to some segments. That entails moving the coverage of some customers from specialty salespeople to generalists, and shifting the coverage of other customers from field salespeople to telesales staff.

As in the maturity stage, companies can shift the selling of easy-to-understand products and the execution of administrative tasks to less expensive resources, such as sales assistants, telesales staff, part-time salespeople, and the Internet.

It's not easy, but a systematic cost-reduction program can help companies live to fight another day. Take the case of an American lubricant manufacturer that in early 2005 needed to cut costs radically to preserve profitability. The company revised its channel strategy, moving the coverage of thousands of customers to selling partners. Those partners had less expensive overheads, such as office space and employee benefits, so their costs were lower than those of the manufacturer. The company shrank its sales force and got the remaining salespeople to focus on selling only to large customers. By the end of the year, the lubricant company had turned the corner.

Sales leaders who try to match sales force structures with the business life cycle face different challenges at every stage. The common thread, though, is that they must overcome organizational resistance at each step and sacrifice short-term profits to secure their companies' success over time.

Originally published in July–August 2006. Reprint R0607F

The End of Solution Sales

by Brent Adamson, Matthew Dixon, and Nicholas Toman

THE HARDEST THING ABOUT B2B selling today is that customers don't need you the way they used to. In recent decades sales reps have become adept at discovering customers' needs and selling them "solutions"—generally, complex combinations of products and services. This worked because customers didn't know how to solve their own problems, even though they often had a good understanding of what their problems were. But now, owing to increasingly sophisticated procurement teams and purchasing consultants armed with troves of data, companies can readily define solutions for themselves.

In fact, a recent Corporate Executive Board study of more than 1,400 B2B customers found that those customers completed, on average, nearly 60% of a typical purchasing decision—researching solutions, ranking options, setting requirements, benchmarking pricing, and so on—before even having a conversation with a supplier. In this world the celebrated "solution sales rep" can be more of an annoyance than an asset. Customers in an array of industries, from IT to insurance to business process outsourcing, are often way ahead of the salespeople who are "helping" them.

But the news is not all bad. Although traditional reps are at a distinct disadvantage in this environment, a select group of high performers are flourishing. These superior reps have abandoned much of the conventional wisdom taught in sales organizations. They:

- evaluate prospects according to criteria different from those used by other reps, targeting agile organizations in a state of flux rather than ones with a clear understanding of their needs
- seek out a very different set of stakeholders, preferring skeptical change agents over friendly informants
- coach those change agents on how to buy, instead of quizzing them about their company's purchasing process

These sales professionals don't just sell more effectively—they sell differently. This means that boosting the performance of average salespeople isn't a matter of *improving* how they currently sell; it involves altogether *changing* how they sell. To accomplish this, organizations need to fundamentally rethink the training and support provided to their reps.

Coming Up Short

Under the conventional solution-selling method that has prevailed since the 1980s, salespeople are trained to align a solution with an acknowledged customer need and demonstrate why it is better than the competition's. This translates into a very practical approach: A rep begins by identifying customers who recognize a problem that the supplier can solve, and gives priority to those who are ready to act. Then, by asking questions, she surfaces a "hook" that enables her to attach her company's solution to that problem. Part and parcel of this approach is her ability to find and nurture somebody within the customer organization—an advocate, or coach—who can help her navigate the company and drive the deal to completion.

But customers have radically departed from the old ways of buying, and sales leaders are increasingly finding that their staffs are relegated to price-driven bake-offs. One CSO at a high-tech organization

Idea in Brief

Sales reps are adept at selling "solutions," but customers have become skilled at finding their own; they don't need reps as they once did. In this environment, a group of high-performing salespeople have emerged—reps who've abandoned the traditional playbook and devised a novel sales strategy.

These reps:

- Look for agile organizations in a state of flux rather than ones with a clear understanding of their needs

- Seek out a very different set of stakeholders, preferring skeptical change agents over friendly informants

- Coach those change agents on how to buy, rather than quizzing them about their company's purchasing process

Unlike traditional solution sellers, these star performers lead with insights meant to upend a customer's approach to its business, and they aren't afraid to push customers out of their comfort zone.

---

told us, "Our customers are coming to the table armed to the teeth with a deep understanding of their problem and a well-scoped RFP for a solution. It's turning many of our sales conversations into fulfillment conversations." Reps must learn to engage customers much earlier, well before customers fully understand their own needs. In many ways, this is a strategy as old as sales itself: To win a deal, you've got to get ahead of the RFP. But our research shows that although that's more important than ever, it's no longer sufficient.

To find out what high-performing sales professionals (defined as those in the top 20% in terms of quota attainment) do differently from other reps, Corporate Executive Board conducted three studies. In the first, we surveyed more than 6,000 reps from 83 companies, spanning every major industry, about how they prioritize opportunities, target and engage stakeholders, and execute the sales process. In the second, we examined complex purchasing scenarios in nearly 600 companies in a variety of industries to understand the various structures and influences of formal and informal buying teams. In the third, we studied more than 700 individual customer stakeholders involved in complex B2B purchases to determine the impact specific kinds of stakeholders can have on organizational buying decisions.

Our key finding: The top-performing reps have abandoned the traditional playbook and devised a novel, even radical, sales approach built on the three strategies outlined above. Let's take a close look at each.

Strategy 1: Avoid the Trap of "Established Demand"

Most organizations tell their salespeople to give priority to customers whose senior management meets three criteria: It has an acknowledged need for change, a clear vision of its goals, and well-established processes for making purchasing decisions. These criteria are easily observable, for the most part, and both reps and their leaders habitually rely on them to predict the likelihood and prog-

A new selling guide for reps

The best salespeople are replacing traditional "solution selling" with "insight selling"—a strategy that demands a radically different approach across several areas of the purchasing process.

Solution selling	Insight selling
What kind of company to target	
Organizations that have a clear vision and established demands	Agile organizations that have emerging demands or are in a state of flux
What sort of initial information to gather	
What need is the customer seeking to address?	What unrecognized need does the customer have?
When to engage	
After the customer has identified a problem the supplier can solve	Before the customer has pinpointed a problem
How to begin the conversation	
Ask questions about the customer's need and look for a "hook" for your solution	Offer provocative insights about what the customer should do
How to direct the flow of information	
Ask questions so that the customer can steer you through its purchasing process	Coach the customer about how to buy, and support it throughout the process

ress of potential deals. Indeed, many companies capture them in a scorecard designed to help reps and managers optimize how they spend their time, allocate specialist support, stage proposals, and improve their forecasts.

Our data, however, show that star performers place little value on such traditional predictors. Instead, they emphasize two nontraditional criteria. First, they put a premium on customer agility: Can a customer act quickly and decisively when presented with a compelling case, or is it hamstrung by structures and relationships that stifle change? Second, they pursue customers that have an emerging need or are in a state of organizational flux, whether because of external pressures, such as regulatory reform, or because of internal pressures, such as a recent acquisition, a leadership turnover, or widespread dissatisfaction with current practices. Since they're already reexamining the status quo, these customers are looking for insights and are naturally more receptive to the disruptive ideas that star performers bring to the table. (See the sidebar "How to Upend Your Customers' Ways of Thinking.") Stars, in other words, place more emphasis on a customer's potential to *change* than on its potential to *buy*. They're able to get in early and advance a disruptive solution because they target accounts where demand is emerging, not established—accounts that are primed for change but haven't yet generated the necessary consensus, let alone settled on a course of action.

One consequence of this orientation is that star performers treat requests for sales presentations very differently than average performers do. Whereas the latter perceive an invitation to present as the best sign of a promising opportunity, the former recognize it for what it is—an invitation to bid for a contract that is probably destined to be awarded to a favored vendor. The star sales rep uses the occasion to reframe the discussion and turn a customer with clearly defined requirements into one with emerging needs. Even when he's invited in late, he tries to rewind the purchasing decision to a much earlier stage.

A sales leader at a business services company recently told us about one of the firm's top sellers, who, asked to give an RFP presentation, quickly commandeered the meeting to his own ends. "Here

How to Upend Your Customers' Ways of Thinking

TRADITIONAL SOLUTION SELLING IS BASED on the premise that salespeople should lead with open-ended questions designed to surface recognized customer needs. Insight-based selling rests on the belief that salespeople must lead with disruptive ideas that will make customers aware of unknown needs.

In *The Challenger Sale* (Portfolio/Penguin, 2011), we draw on data from more than 6,000 salespeople around the world to show that all reps fall into one of five profiles—the Relationship Builder, the Reactive Problem Solver, the Hard Worker, the Lone Wolf, and the Challenger. Star performers are far more likely to be Challengers than any other type. Why? Challengers are the debaters on the sales team. They've got a provocative point of view that can upend a customer's current practices, and they're not afraid to push customers outside their comfort zone. (This idea was explored by Philip Lay, Todd Hewlin, and Geoffrey Moore in the March 2009 HBR article "In a Downturn, Provoke Your Customers.")

Challengers accounted for nearly 40% of the high performers in our study—and the number jumps to 54% in complex, insight-driven environments. Customers value the Challenger approach; in a corollary study, we found that the biggest driver of B2B customer loyalty is a supplier's ability to deliver new insights.

Getting the Challenger approach right requires organizational capabilities as well as individual skills. While salespeople need to be comfortable with the tension inherent in a teaching-oriented sales conversation, sales and marketing leaders must create teachable insights for them to deliver in the first

is our full response to your RFP—everything you were looking for," he told the assembled executives. "However, because we have only 60 minutes together, I'm going to let you read that on your own. I'd like to use our time to walk you through the three things we believe *should* have been in the RFP but weren't, and to explain why they matter so much." At the end of the meeting the customer sent home the two vendors who were still waiting for their turn, canceled the RFP process, and started over: The rep had made it clear to the executives that they were asking the wrong questions. He reshaped the deal to align with his company's core capabilities and ultimately place. When handled skillfully, those insights guide the conversation toward areas where the supplier outperforms its competitors.

The Challenger approach is becoming standard operating procedure in top sales organizations. Reps for Dentsply International, a global provider of dental products and services, talk to dentists about hygienists' absences from work related to carpal tunnel syndrome and similar injuries. They demonstrate how Dentsply's lighter, cordless hygiene equipment may reduce wrist stress. Salespeople for the agricultural products and services firm Cargill discuss how price volatility in international markets causes farmers to waste time trying to predict commodity price shifts. The subject naturally leads to a pitch for grain-pricing services, which help farmers mitigate their exposure to price fluctuations.

Instead of leading with a discussion about the technical benefits of their products, account teams at Ciena, a global provider of telecommunications equipment, software, and services, focus the conversation on the business benefits, such as reducing operational inefficiencies in networks. For example, they talk about how much money the customer could save by eliminating unnecessary service calls through improved network automation. And reps for the food services company Aramark use insights gleaned from serving one consumer segment (say, college students) to change the way prospective customers in other segments think about managing their business (for example, how the military feeds its members).

—B.A. and M.D.

landed it. Like other star performers, he knew that the way in was not to try to meet the customer's existing needs but to redefine them. Instead of taking a conventional solution-sales approach, he used an "insight selling" strategy, revealing to the customer needs it didn't know it had.

Research in practice
Drawing on data that include interviews with nearly 100 high performers worldwide, we developed a new scorecard that managers can use to coach their reps and help them adopt the criteria and

approaches that star performers focus on. (See the exhibit "Prioritizing your opportunities.") One industrial automation company we've worked with has effectively employed it, with a few tweaks to account for industry idiosyncrasies. When its managers sit down with reps to prioritize activity and assess opportunities, the scorecard gives them a concrete way to redirect average performers toward opportunities they might otherwise overlook or underpursue and to steer the conversation naturally toward seeking out emerging demand. (A word of caution: Formal scorecards can give rise to bureaucratic, overengineered processes for evaluating prospects. Sales leaders should use them as conversation starters and coaching guides, not inviolable checklists.)

Strategy 2: Target Mobilizers, Not Advocates

As we noted earlier, in conventional sales training reps are taught to find an advocate, or coach, within the customer organization to help them get the deal done. They're given a laundry list of attributes to look for. The description below, compiled from dozens of companies' training materials, suggests that the ideal advocate:

- is accessible and willing to meet when asked
- provides valuable information that's typically unavailable to outside suppliers
- is predisposed to support the supplier's solution
- is good at influencing others
- speaks the truth
- is considered credible by colleagues
- conveys new ideas to colleagues in savvy, persuasive ways
- delivers on commitments
- stands to personally gain from the sale
- will help reps network and connect with other stakeholders

Prioritizing your opportunities

The scorecard below, derived from the ways high-performing reps evaluate potential customers, can help you assess whether or not to pursue a deal.

1. Organizational basics	Yes	No		
Does the customer have significant current or potential spend?	☐	☐		If either answer is no, do not pursue a deal
Is the customer financially sound?	☐	☐		

2. Operating environment	Yes	No	Unknown	
Does the customer face external pressures to change, such as new industry regulations or loss of market position?	☐	☐	☐	1 point for each Yes
Are there internal pressures to change, such as new management or a rethinking of strategic direction?	☐	☐	☐	

3. View of the status quo	Yes	No	Unknown	
Is there organization-wide discontent with the status quo?	☐	☐	☐	2 points for each Yes
Does the current supplier fall short of expectations?	☐	☐	☐	
Is the customer unhappy with existing workarounds?	☐	☐	☐	

4. Receptivity to new or disruptive ideas	Yes	No	Unknown	
Do internal stakeholders frequently share best practices?	☐	☐	☐	3 points for each Yes
Do they attend conferences and other learning events?	☐	☐	☐	
Do leaders look to the broader organization for ideas?	☐	☐	☐	

5. Potential for emerging needs	Yes	No	Unknown	
Do stakeholders engage in constructive dialogue when their assumptions are challenged?	☐	☐	☐	4 points for each Yes
Do they seek to continue conversations about industry benchmarks and trends?	☐	☐	☐	
Is there at least one confirmed "Mobilizer" in the company?	☐	☐	☐	

Total ☐

Scoring

0–10
Consider not pursuing the opportunity

10–20
Consider pursuing with limited resources

20+
Consider pursuing with limited resources

Don't Target Talkers

BEING A MOBILIZER HAS LITTLE to do with function, role, or seniority. High-level decision makers are just as likely to be Talkers or Blockers. The peril for most reps is that their instinct tells them to target Talkers. And they view a senior-level Talker, such as a CEO or a CFO, as the holy grail—someone who holds the purse strings and is eager to meet. But these decision makers are often unwilling or unable to build the consensus needed for large-scale change—so what seems like an "ideal deal" is more likely to head to the graveyard than to the income statement.

We heard the same list, or a variation on it, from sales leaders and trainers the world over. It turns out, though, that this idealized advocate doesn't actually exist. Each attribute can probably be found somewhere in a customer organization, but our research shows that the traits rarely all come together in one person. So reps find themselves settling for someone who has *some* of them. And when choosing an advocate, we've found, most reps walk right past the very people who could help them get the deal done—the people star performers have learned to recognize and rely on.

In our survey of customer stakeholders, we asked them to assess themselves according to 135 attributes and perspectives. Our analysis revealed seven distinct stakeholder profiles and measured the relative ability of individuals of each type to build consensus and drive action around a large corporate purchase or initiative. The profiles aren't mutually exclusive; most people have attributes of more than one. Still, the data clearly show that virtually every stakeholder has a primary posture when it comes to working with suppliers and spearheading organizational change.

Here are the seven profiles we identified.

1. **Go-Getters.** Motivated by organizational improvement and constantly looking for good ideas, Go-Getters champion action around great insights wherever they find them.
2. **Teachers.** Passionate about sharing insights, Teachers are sought out by colleagues for their input. They're especially good at persuading others to take a specific course of action.

3. **Skeptics.** Wary of large, complicated projects, Skeptics push back on almost everything. Even when championing a new idea, they counsel careful, measured implementation.
4. **Guides.** Willing to share the organization's latest gossip, Guides furnish information that's typically unavailable to outsiders.
5. **Friends.** Just as nice as the name suggests, Friends are readily accessible and will happily help reps network with other stakeholders in the organization.
6. **Climbers.** Focused primarily on personal gain, Climbers back projects that will raise their own profiles, and they expect to be rewarded when those projects succeed.
7. **Blockers.** Perhaps better described as "anti-stakeholders," Blockers are strongly oriented toward the status quo. They have little interest in speaking with outside vendors.

Our research also reveals that average reps gravitate toward three stakeholder profiles, and star reps gravitate toward three others. Average reps typically connect with Guides, Friends, and Climbers—types that we group together as Talkers. These people are personable and accessible and they share company information freely, all of which makes them very appealing. But if your goal is to close a deal, not just have a chat, Talkers won't get you very far: They're often poor at building the consensus necessary for complex purchasing decisions. Ironically, traditional sales training pushes reps into the arms of Talkers—thus reinforcing the very underperformance companies seek to improve.

The profiles that star reps pursue—Go-Getters, Teachers, and Skeptics—are far better at generating consensus. We refer to them as Mobilizers. A conversation with a Mobilizer isn't necessarily easy. Because Mobilizers are focused first and foremost on driving productive change for their company, that's what they want to talk about—*their* company, not yours. In fact, in many ways Mobilizers are deeply supplier-agnostic. They're less likely to get behind a particular supplier than behind a particular insight. Reps who rely on a traditional features-and-benefits sales approach will probably fail to engage Mobilizers.

Endless questioning and needs diagnosis are of no value to Mobilizers. They don't want to be asked what keeps them awake at night; they're looking for outside experts to share insights about what their company should do, and they're engaged by big, disruptive ideas. Yet upon hearing those ideas, Mobilizers ask a lot of tough questions—Go-Getters because they want to *do,* Teachers because they want to *share,* and Skeptics because they want to *test.* Skeptics are especially likely to pick apart an insight before moving forward. That can be intimidating for most reps, who are apt to mistake the Skeptic's interrogation for hostility rather than engagement. But star performers live for this kind of conversation. We spoke with one who said, "If the customer isn't skeptical and doesn't push me, then either I've done something wrong or she just isn't serious."

Research in practice
We worked with star reps around the world to develop a practical guide to identifying Mobilizers. (See the exhibit "Finding the right allies.") The first step is to gauge a customer's reaction to a provocative insight. (For instance, reps at the industrial supply company Grainger start their conversations by citing data showing that a shockingly high share—40%—of companies' spend on maintenance, repair, and operations goes to unplanned purchases.) Does the customer dismiss the insight out of hand, accept it at face value, or test it with hard questions? Contrary to conventional wisdom, hard questions are a good sign; they suggest that the contact has the healthy skepticism of a Mobilizer. If the customer accepts the assertion without question, you've got a Talker or a Blocker—the difference being that a Talker will at least offer useful information about his organization, whereas a Blocker will not engage in dialogue at all.

Next, the rep must listen carefully to *how* the customer discusses the insight as the conversation progresses. Watch out for the customer who says something like "You're preaching to the converted. I've been lobbying for this sort of thing for years!" If he sees the idea

THE END OF SOLUTION SALES

Finding the right allies

We identified seven distinct stakeholder profiles within customer organizations. Star reps filter out the less useful types and target the ones who could help drive the deal. Here's how to do the same.

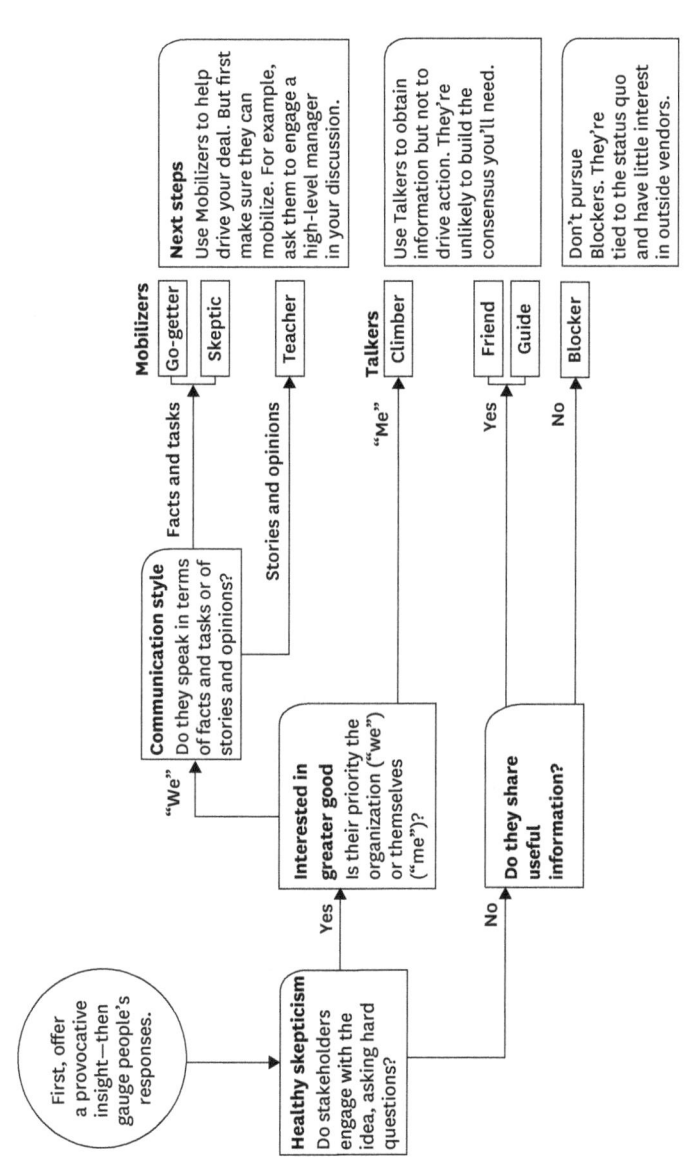

as a means of advancing his personal agenda—speaking mainly in terms of "me" versus "we"—that's a strong signal that he's a Climber. And Climbers can be dangerous. A number of star reps told us that Climbers aren't obvious just to them; they're obvious to colleagues and often cause widespread resentment and distrust.

Star performers never assume they've identified a Mobilizer until that person has proved it with her actions. Stars usually ask stakeholders they believe might be Mobilizers to set up a meeting with key decision makers or to provide information obtainable only by actively investigating an issue or conferring with colleagues. One star performer from a global telecommunications company explained to us that she always tests what her customer contacts tell her they can do. In particular, she asks them to invite senior decision makers, often from other functions, to follow-on meetings. If they fail to get the right people to attend, she knows that although they may *aspire* to mobilize, they probably lack the connections or the clout to actually do so.

Strategy 3: Coach Customers on How to Buy

Sales leaders often overlook the fact that as hard as it is for most suppliers to sell complex solutions, it's even harder for most customers to buy them. This is especially true when Mobilizers take the lead, because they're "idea people" who tend to be far less familiar than Talkers with the ins and outs of internal purchasing processes.

Having watched similar deals go off the rails in other organizations, suppliers are frequently better positioned than the customer to steer a purchase through the organization. Suppliers can foresee likely objections. They can anticipate cross-silo politicking. And in many cases they can head off problems before they arise. The process is part of the overarching strategy of providing insight rather than extracting it. Whereas most reps rely on a customer to coach them through a sale, stars coach the customer.

In light of this fact, it's instructive to reflect on how much time and effort sales organizations invest in equipping their reps to "discover" the customer's purchasing process. Most carefully train them to ask a host of questions about how decisions are made and how the deal is likely to progress, assuming that the customer will have accurate answers. That's a poor strategy. Sales leaders find this notion deeply unsettling. How can a rep guide a customer through the purchasing process when he probably doesn't understand the idiosyncrasies of the customer's organization? Isn't each customer's buying process unique? In a word, no. One star rep we interviewed explained, "I don't waste a lot of time asking my customers about who has to be involved in the vetting process, whose buy-in we need to obtain, or who holds the purse strings. The customers won't know—they're new to this kind of purchase. In the majority of my deals, I know more about how the purchase will unfold than the customers do. I let them champion the vision internally, but it's my job to help them get the deal done."

Research in practice

Automatic Data Processing (ADP), a global leader in business outsourcing solutions, recently introduced a methodology designed to reorient its sales reps—and the entire company—around its customers' purchasing processes. It's called Buying Made Easy.

The goal is to reduce the burden on the customer by having sales reps follow prescribed steps, each with its own tools and documents to support customers throughout the process. Instead of representing a set of sales activities, as in traditional programs, the steps represent a set of buying activities ("recognize need," "evaluate options," "validate and select a solution") along with recommended actions that will help salespeople guide the customer. Any conversation at ADP about the status of a deal takes into account what the customer has to do next and how ADP can help make that happen.

In addition, ADP has created verification steps to ensure that reps can accurately and fully document the customer's purchasing progress. One verifier, for example, is the customer's written commitment to run a presales diagnostic assessing the company's exposure to risk and its readiness to move to an outsourced solution. Each verifier is a clear, objective indicator of exactly where a customer is in the purchasing process.

It's the end of traditional solution selling. Customers are increasingly circumventing reps; they're using publicly available information to diagnose their own needs and turning to sophisticated procurement departments and third-party purchasing consultants to help them extract the best possible deals from suppliers. The trend will only accelerate. For sales, this isn't just another long, hot summer; it's wholesale climate change.

Many reps will simply ignore the upheaval and stick with solution selling, and their customers will increasingly rebuff them. But adaptive reps, who seek out customers that are primed for change, challenge them with provocative insights, and coach them on how to buy, will become indispensable. They may still be selling solutions—but more broadly, they're selling insights. And in this new world, that makes the difference between a pitch that goes nowhere and one that secures the customer's business.

Originally published in July–August 2012. Reprint R1207C

Selling into Micromarkets

by Manish Goyal, Maryanne Q. Hancock, and Homayoun Hatami

FOR YEARS, SALES REPS at a leading chemicals and services company had successfully worked their territories, but in recent months sales volume had plateaued, because of encroaching competitors and shifting demand. Using its emerging analytics capability, the global firm took a more granular look at its business. It diced its seven U.S. regions into 70 "micromarkets" and zeroed in on those with the greatest potential. It then pulled reps away from overserved territories, created sales "plays" for the newly identified hot spots, and redeployed the sales force. Within a year the sales growth rate doubled—without an increase in marketing or sales costs.

The key to the firm's remarkable turnaround was its new ability to combine, sift, and sort vast troves of data to develop a highly efficient sales strategy. While B2C companies have become adept at mining the petabytes of transactional and other purchasing data that consumers generate as they interact online, B2B sales organizations have only recently begun to use big data to both inform overall strategy and tailor sales pitches for specific customers in real time. Yet the payoff can be huge: As a sales executive at the chemicals company told us, "There's no need to rely on intuition and guesswork anymore."

To understand how sales organizations are beginning to use big data, we interviewed 120 sales executives at a range of companies around the world that have significantly outperformed their peers in revenue and profitability. These in-depth conversations suggest that micromarket strategy is perhaps the most potent new application of big-data analytics in B2B sales. While micromarkets are most often understood as physical regions, they needn't always be; as we'll describe even an air-cargo route can be a micromarket. Discovering and exploiting new-growth hot spots involves three steps: Defining your micromarkets and determining their growth potential; using these findings to distribute resources and guide the sales force; and incorporating the big-data mind-set into operations and organizational culture.

Let's look at each in turn.

Find New Pockets of Growth

Many companies believe that they have a good understanding of the growth prospects for their sales regions or territories, but until sales leaders dice that geography into dozens or hundreds of micromarkets, they will be unable to see which counties, zip codes, or other circumscribed areas are underexploited and which are unlikely to grow. What's more, they will not have a clear idea of whether they're deploying their sales force to the greatest effect.

The first step in pursuing a micromarket strategy is to create an "opportunity map" of potentially lucrative hot spots. (See the sidebar "Five Steps to Finding Pockets of Growth" for a step-by-step discussion.) The map taps internal and external data sets from a variety of sources and uses sophisticated analytics to build a picture of the future opportunity, not the historical reality—a key to positioning the sales force for success.

To paint this high-resolution picture, a company starts by determining the ideal size and positions of its micromarkets, given the firm's goals and resources. Next, managers examine what drives customers' purchasing in each market, determine the firm's

Idea in Brief

Sophisticated sales organizations are combining and crunching the mountains of data now available about customers, competitors, and their own operations to dice up their existing sales regions into dozens or hundreds of "micromarkets" and identify new-growth hot spots.

Micromarket analyses proceed through five steps: defining the optimal micromarket size; determining the growth potential for each; gauging the market share in each; understanding the causes of variation in market share; and prioritizing high-potential markets to focus on.

Micromarket strategies work only if sales teams have simple tools that make them easy to implement, in particular, tailored sales "plays" for the opportunities similar micromarkets represent. These strategies require new types of cross-functional collaboration—for instance, between sales and marketing, which have to function as a single team.

---

current market share in each, and look for causes of the variance among markets. On the basis of that analysis, the company identifies which markets represent the greatest growth opportunities.

Given the complexity of the data gathering and analysis that these tasks entail, it is far more efficient to bring sales and marketing together to create a micromarket map than to have dispersed groups across functions pursuing pieces and then trying to cobble them together into a coherent picture. The goal is to define the problem, the methods for solving it, and, crucially, how to translate the resulting insights into tools the sales team can use.

Make It Easy for the Sales Team

For a micromarket strategy to work, management must have the courage and imagination to act on the insights revealed by the analysis. Most sales leaders deploy resources on the basis of the current or historical performance of a given sales region. We believe that while going after future opportunities at the micromarket level can seem risky, basing strategy on old views of markets and their past performance is riskier still.

Five Steps to Finding Pockets of Growth

BUILDCO, A BUILDING PRODUCTS COMPANY, identified lucrative hot spots in its Texas market through a five-step process. (This fictionalized example draws on the experience of a large U.S.-based B2B company we worked with.)

An opportunity map is the foundation of micromarket strategy. Here's a closer look at each step in the process.

1. Define Micromarket Size

Start by determining the optimal size for your micromarkets. Should they be delineated by county, zip code, or something else? To answer this question, gauge your reps' territory radius—the average distance they travel from a central point in the field. Choosing a size smaller than the territory radius would underutilize the sales force. Next, identify the points at which market dynamics shift—for example, at the limits of a competitor's region or the boundary where customer density changes. Finally, determine whether the sales force will be able to execute effectively. A county-level micromarket may seem ideal from a strategic standpoint, but the sales force may lack the resources or capability to cover a region of that size.

Using factors such as reps' territory radius as a guide, BuildCo segmented its 10 Texas sales regions into 254 counties, each one a micromarket.

2. Determine Growth Potential

To gauge each micromarket's growth potential, determine what drives your customers' (and potential customers') purchases. Build a list of 15 to 20 drivers using industry knowledge, interviews with customers and reps, and informed hypotheses. Drivers might include cost of inputs, cost of capital, local demographics, and so on. Determine to what degree each driver influences customer purchases—for instance, derive simple correlations of growth using historical data from the previous two or three years. Understanding which drivers have the greatest influence on customer demand helps you determine in which micromarkets future growth is most likely. Also, information about demand at the individual customer level, when aggregated, can help further define high-growth geographic areas.

By examining the drivers of customer purchasing in each micromarket, such as terrain and age of housing stock, the firm gauged which markets were most likely to grow.

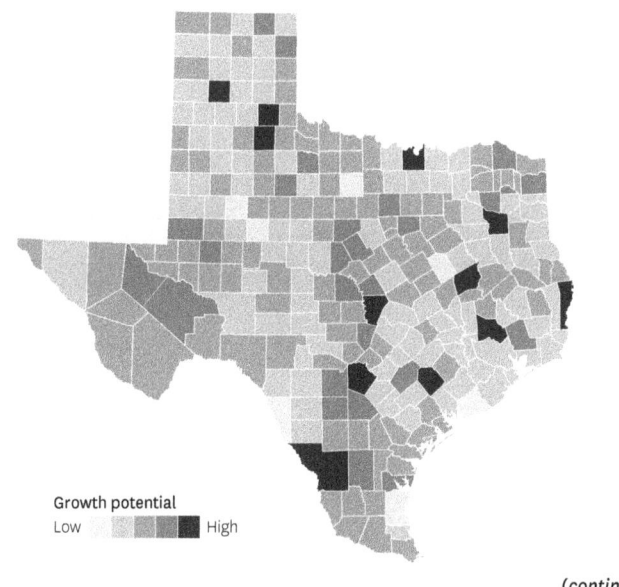

(*continued*)

3. Gauge Market Share

Using sales data, determine market share for each micromarket. The key data are revenues and margins across lines of business. Often this step is a sticking point for companies because they don't have ready access to data at this level.

Next, calculate sales trends in each micromarket for the previous two or three quarters—or two or three years for seasonal businesses—and compare them with data from your opportunity map. This will show how your market share is trending. Market share often varies fivefold or more among micromarkets; share-of-growth may vary by twice that.

BuildCo determined that market share was far from uniform across micromarkets, varying as much as fivefold.

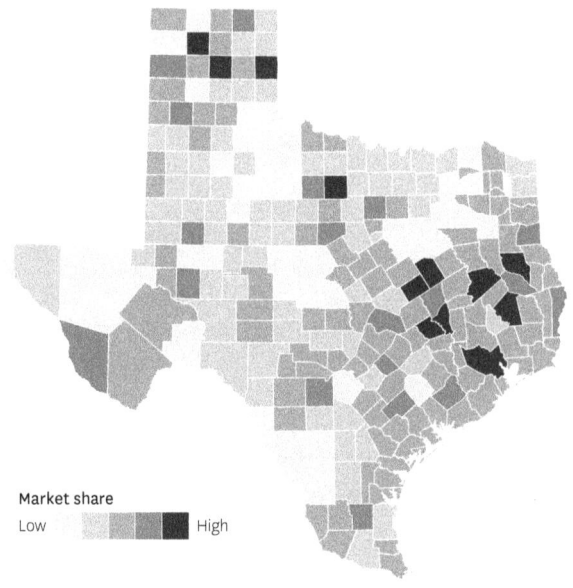

4. Identify the Causes of Differences in Market Share

Next, determine what accounts for the variations in your share across micromarkets. Collect internal and external data on the marketing and sales activities that could impact market share. These commonly include data on reps' coverage of each market and their quotas and performance within each; related data for your partners in the market; your marketing spend; and pricing by channel and by product. The key is to understand how both your sales strategy and competitive factors affect market share in each micromarket.

Then determine whether variations in these levers account for variation in market share. For example, in a micromarket where you have a low market share, is inadequate rep coverage to blame, or are shifting demographics causing the poor performance?

Sales leaders identified the main causes of low market share in high-growth-potential micromarkets. Low rep coverage and low marketing spend were the easiest and most effective to address.

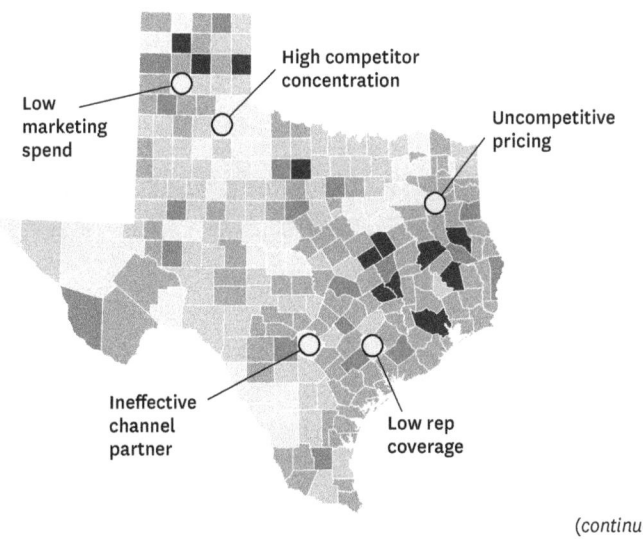

(continued)

5. Prioritize Growth Pockets

Understanding root causes of market share variance allows you to prioritize your micromarkets and determine which growth pockets to focus on. For example, companies might want to direct resources to areas having more-easily addressed causes of low market share, such as poor sales rep coverage, rather than areas where the cause is, say, uncompetitive pricing if their cost structure would make a price war hard to win.

Prioritizing micromarkets is an iterative exercise. Senior management develops top-down guidelines for the approach to each peer group of micromarkets. To ensure buy-in from the field, it's important that sales managers have the flexibility to maneuver at a local level in, say, deciding how many reps and which ones will move from a low-priority area to a hot spot.

On the basis of the analysis, BuildCo moved more reps and marketing dollars to the top 20% of the high-growth/low-market-share micromarkets while keeping total spend constant.

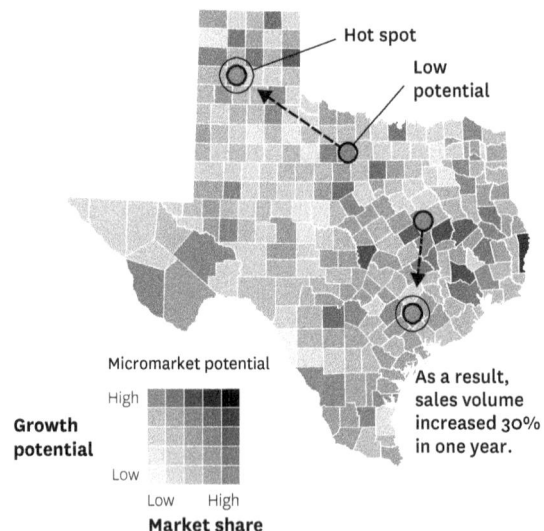

Once management is on board, the sales team needs to understand the rationale behind the micromarket strategy and have simple tools that make it easy to implement. That means aligning sales coverage with opportunity and creating straightforward sales "plays" for each type of opportunity.

Align sales coverage with opportunity

During the annual sales-planning process, managers determine how to invest resources to capture anticipated demand. The first step is to overlay the rough allocation of resources across markets on the basis of their overall potential. But instead of then applying salespeople consistently across customers, managers use insights about growth opportunities and recommended coverage models for various market types to fundamentally rethink their reps' distribution.

For example, a high-growth urban pocket with low competitive intensity where a company does not have much coverage should add "hunter" capacity; depending on customer density, that market might be able to sustain a few such reps, each specializing in a particular set of customer segments. A lower-growth market where the company has significant share would require "defensive farming"— that is, fewer reps, but with strong skills in account management. Local sales managers should be trained on how to use the data from the opportunity map to identify more precisely where they want their reps to spend their time and how they want to size their territories.

Consider the case of the chemicals company. Instead of looking at current sales by region, as it had always done, the company examined market share within customer industry sectors in specific U.S. counties. The micromarket analysis revealed that although the company had 20% of the overall market, it had up to 60% in some markets but as little as 10% in others, including some of the fastest-growing segments. On the basis of this analysis, the company redeployed its sales force to exploit the growth.

For instance, one sales rep had been spending more than half her time 200 miles from her home office, even though only a quarter of her region's opportunity lay there. This was purely because sales

What Is Big Data?

"BIG DATA" REFERS TO VAST DATA sets typically collected in multiple forms from many sources, often in real time. In B2B contexts these data may be pulled from social networks, e-commerce sites, customer call records, and many other sources. These aren't the regular data sets that companies have in their CRM databases. Ranging from a few dozen terabytes to many petabytes, they're so extensive and complex that specialized software tools and analytics expertise are required to collect, manage, and mine them. They can be used for everything from extracting sales insights from unstructured data (such as comments about particular brands on the internet) to assessing regional weather patterns to predict beer consumption to understanding the competitive landscape at a granular level.

---

territories had been assigned according to historical performance rather than growth prospects. Now she spends 75% of her time in an area where 75% of the opportunity exists—within 50 miles of her office. Changes like these increased the firm's growth rate of new accounts from 15% to 25% in just one year.

Create sales plays for each type of opportunity
Micromarket analyses present myriad new opportunities, so the challenge for companies is how to help a generalist sales force effectively tailor messaging and materials to the opportunity.

Companies should identify groups of micromarkets—or "peer groups"—that share certain characteristics. For example, one peer group might be high-growth micromarkets with limited competitive intensity. Another might be made up of markets with similar operating cost structures. Because they are structurally similar, peer groups represent similar sales opportunities. Companies usually find that a set of four to 10 peer groups is a manageable number.

For each peer group, marketing managers develop the strategy and "play"—the best way to sell into that set of customers or market. For example, the chemicals company grouped its 70 micromarkets into four peer groups and outlined a strategy for each, such as "invest," in which it sought to capture an outsize share of growth, or "maintain," in which it sought to hold on to its market share while maximizing operating efficiencies. The play usually encompasses guidance on the offer, pricing, and communications and may include tailored collateral materials.

Companies typically devise and perfect plays either by adapting approaches that have been successful in similar settings or by testing new plays in pilot markets. One telecommunications company we spoke with continually tested plays on different customer segments to determine which offers at which price points with which types of services were most successful in various markets.

Finally, sales managers communicate to the field sales force the rationale for how markets or customers have been assigned to the peer groups and the strategies and plays for each group. This transparency will be important in motivating reps and helping them understand performance expectations, as we'll discuss further on.

All this came together in the case of a cargo airline that used micromarket strategy with great success. In an innovative move, this airline delineated micromarkets not by geographic area but according to flight paths—regarding each route as a micromarket. It then gauged demand in each one—looking at variables such as volume and timing—and sorted customers into peer groups. One customer, for example, needed to ship fresh sea bass from Italy on Wednesdays for weekend consumption in New York. For another customer, a commercial greenhouse, peak demand occurred during the week before Valentine's Day.

Drawing on this analysis, the company developed a different negotiation play for each peer group. For instance, it could increase prices for customers that shipped at high-demand times or on high-demand routes, and it could relax volume commitments for customers shipping on lower-demand routes. It could also adjust pricing according to how much capacity was available on a given flight or route and could recognize which customers were contributing more within challenging micromarkets and target—and reward—them accordingly.

Support the sales force in executing the plays

For a micromarket strategy to succeed, the sales training has to be experiential. Salespeople should engage with the opportunity maps that reveal hot (and cool) micromarkets in a given geography and test their intuition against hard data. (It can be eye-opening for them to discover that data analysis is often superior to anecdote in this realm.) Training should also allow them to act out and hone the recommended sales plays. Not only does this hands-on engagement help win over sales reps, but it's a much more effective teaching method than lectures or demonstrations.

In addition to interactive training, reps will need direct coaching on specific pitches. To this end, several leading companies have created in-house "win labs" in which sales and marketing experts help reps craft their pitches. (The opportunity map, devised early in a micromarket analysis, provides invaluable information because it reveals drivers of demand: what makes a given customer buy.) Salespeople are required to bring their pitch plans to the win lab—usually virtually—and the lab team provides data, insights, and value-proposition collateral about the market or similar customers that the rep can use to create a sales play for a specific customer.

For example, our chemicals company produced pitch packs for each industry it served. The packs were further customized for the decision maker with whom the sales rep would interact. "Previously my documents looked like chicken scratch," one rep eloquently put it. "Now I have slick, tailored materials ranging from a four-page summary for the factory manager to a more in-depth technical document for the R&D manager."

Obviously, supporting the sales team to execute on micromarket strategies is not a onetime effort; management must create ongoing support capabilities. For instance, at the air cargo company, management developed a simple performance dashboard to help reps manage pricing and volume negotiations with large customers by route, time, capacity, and competition. The dashboard includes critical real-time information, such as whether the specific flight is overbooked, as well as information on the weekly itineraries of the airline and its competitors. The sales manager holds weekly sales strategy discussions with each rep to ensure that he or she is well positioned to negotiate the best deals. This effort has generated an average increase in share of wallet as high as 20% to 50% with key customers.

Put Data at the Heart of Sales

To sustain the early wins from a micromarket strategy, companies need to change their approach to sales force management in three ways: They must rethink performance management, open new channels between sales and marketing, and invest in talent development.

Performance management

Few managerial moves will kill new initiatives faster than continuing to reward old behaviors. As a start, managers must shift from

How data can drive sales growth

Traditional approach	Micromarket strategy
Data management	
Sales collects customer data from internal sources (CRM, billing, customer-service databases)	Sales combines very large databases of internal and external data such as demographics, social media chatter, and competitive intensity
Data are updated and analyzed quarterly or semi-annually	Data are updated and analyzed monthly, weekly, and daily
Outside analysts provide tools, advice, and statistical services	Data collection and analytics are done by in-house experts
Resource allocation	
Sales coverage is defined by large regions and territories	Sales coverage is segmented into dozens or hundreds of micromarkets
Sales resources are allocated according to a region's historical performance	Resources are deployed at the micromarket level according to expected future opportunity
Performance management	
Rep (and channel partner) performance is assessed relative to other reps (and other channel partners)	Performance is assessed relative to the opportunity within micromarkets
Collaboration	
Sales, marketing, and other departments are siloed	Sales, marketing, strategy, customer service, and other functions are collaborative

assessing reps' performance relative to the entire sales force to assessing it relative to the opportunity. You don't necessarily want Mary to try to outperform James; you want her to hit or surpass a target you set on the basis of the micromarkets and peer group she's selling to.

Performance management in a data-rich sales environment can get closer than ever before to measuring true performance of a sales force. An age-old source of frustration (and skewed impressions) is that a great salesperson in a declining market may be working miracles but she will look like she's underperforming if she's measured against historical data or colleagues who cover growing markets. By sorting micromarkets or customer sets into peer groups according to the future sales opportunity they represent, companies can create better-informed sales plans and targets. They also can, finally, compare apples with apples by looking at sales performance among reps working the same peer group and evaluating the reps against carefully considered targets for that group, rather than against arbitrary growth numbers.

Cross-functional collaboration

In micromarket-focused organizations, marketing often takes on an expanded role, particularly in providing sales with data analytics and supporting the development and testing of sales plays for a specific micromarket or customer peer group.

Consider the case of an Asian telecommunications company that found through a micromarket analysis that 20% of its marketing budget was being squandered in markets with the lowest lifetime customer value. The firm shifted these funds to its most lucrative markets, where two-thirds of the opportunity lay. Marketing then partnered with sales to reset customer-acquisition goals at the micromarket level, on the basis of each market's potential; previously, the goals had been uniform across markets. In the past, when marketing opaquely set targets, sales would treat them skeptically and try to lower them; but under the new micromarket strategy, marketing collaborated with sales to set targets in a transparent way. Far from pushing back on targets, sales sought quotas 10% higher than those of the previous year—and met them.

Using Big Data to Target Individual Prospects

MICROMARKET ANALYSES ARE POWERFUL TOOLS for identifying granular growth opportunities and promising sales areas overlooked by competitors, but knowing which accounts within each micromarket are the best prospects turns a broad target into a narrow bull's-eye.

To tailor offers, communications, and pricing, companies must seek data on potential customers' specific characteristics, such as purchase history and service experience, satisfaction with offerings, and actual use patterns. For example, an agricultural equipment manufacturer that had divided its sales regions into micromarkets realized that its sales teams had relatively little insight into individual end users' needs other than what they gleaned from focus groups, which often included "friendly" customers. The sales teams set out to collect and combine large data sets from partners about the ordering patterns of individuals and groups of customers and their geographies and then developed hypotheses about purchasing behavior for each peer group.

Building on its success in exploiting purchasing data, the company piloted a more audacious initiative that used remote sensing data to determine individual farmers' activities. This provided the insights for sales programs tailored for individual farmers according to the types of crops they had under cultivation. This required sophisticated analytics, but the payoff was significant.

Some B2B firms use social media analytics to create highly targeted lead lists. One tech company, for example, identified keywords or search terms that signaled sales opportunities (for example, queries about how to use specific products or applications). Data scientists tracked IT managers using the keywords on Twitter, Quora, LinkedIn, and Facebook in real time and determined their location (using either IP address or public mobile phone location data). The location data was matched with internal data to place the people at specific companies. Those leads were then sent to the reps with a simplified set of sales insights related to the specific questions posted on social media. Sales reps converted these solid leads almost 80% of the time.

Given the historical tension between marketing and sales, management must establish clear, standardized processes at key bridge points. These include data handoffs and feedback loops that, for example, allow for insights provided by marketing to be tested by sales in the field and for the results to be returned to marketing to guide further research and analytics.

But this arms-length interaction doesn't maximize the potential of true collaboration. What's ultimately needed is to put marketing and sales in the same boat, as some of the most progressive organizations have, where they learn to function as a team. One way to do this is to formally (and physically) combine marketing and sales on certain tasks, as win labs do. Another is to hold marketing accountable for sales growth, an effective and increasingly common arrangement.

Talent development
To take advantage of the opportunities offered by micromarket strategy, both marketing and sales teams will need to step up their capabilities, particularly with analytic talent. That will be a challenge. The McKinsey Global Institute reports that by 2018, U.S. companies alone may face a shortage of up to 190,000 people with deep analytic skills as well as 1.5 million managers and analysts with the know-how to use big-data analysis to make good decisions. And yet the most effective sales organizations will be those that put data analytics at the center of their strategies.

The critical component in this talent equation is the bridge between analysis and action. While analytic talent is important, the best sales leaders put equal emphasis on translating the analysts' insights into guidance that the field can act on. High-performing companies typically embed a few experienced and respected sales managers in the analytics team. They function as a link to the field and translate insights into language the field can follow and spread as best practices across markets. Some companies identify a few talented salespeople who are strong problem solvers, ground them in data methodologies, and challenge them to come up with innovative plays that take full advantage of big data. The firms follow through by funding their pilot ideas. This sort of frontline talent and capability building is essential and will produce the kind of inventive thinkers that are critical to creating successful micromarket strategies.

Finding growth with big data is more than an add-on; it affects every aspect of a business, requiring a change in mind-set from leadership down to the front lines. This is a theme that echoed across our conversations with sales executives around the world. Describing such a transformation at Pioneer Hi-Bred, a DuPont agricultural products company, Alejandro Munoz, the vice president for the Americas and global production, told us, "This granular view is really a new way of thinking . . . and it takes time for it to become part of the company's DNA." At Pioneer, it took years, he said, but today it guides "how we run our commercial operations, how we invest against opportunities, and how we deploy sales and marketing."

Micromarket strategies are demanding, but they consistently give sales a competitive edge. Sales leaders should ask whether they can afford not to embrace big data.

Originally published in July–August 2012. Reprint R1207F

Dismantling the Sales Machine

by Brent Adamson, Matthew Dixon,
and Nicholas Toman

SALES LEADERS HAVE LONG FIXATED on process discipline. They have created opportunity scorecards, qualification criteria, and activity metrics—all part of a formal sales process designed to help their team members replicate the approaches of star performers. This is the world of the sales machine, built to outsell less focused, less disciplined competitors through brute efficiency and world-class tools and training.

For years, tuning this machine has been the primary means of boosting sales productivity. But recently sales has been caught off guard by a dramatic shift in customers' buying behavior. Even as leadership has tightened compliance with the processes that have served so well, sales performance has grown increasingly erratic. Companies are reporting longer sales cycle times, lower conversion rates, less reliable forecasts, and compressed margins. The sales machine is stalling.

The good news is that the way forward is clear. In our research at CEB, we have found that the very approaches that made the sales machine so effective now make selling harder. We have also identified the keys to winning in this new environment: Leaders must abandon their fixation on process compliance and embrace a flexible approach to selling driven by sales reps' reliance on insight and judgment.

The Rise of Insight Selling

Until recently, customers seeking business solutions had to ask suppliers for guidance early in the purchasing process, because crucial information wasn't available anywhere else. But today customers are better informed than ever before. By the time they approach suppliers, they generally have a clear idea of the problem they need to solve, the solutions that are available, and the price they're willing to pay. In this world, process-driven sales machine approaches fall short, because they give sales reps no room to exercise judgment and creativity in dealing with highly knowledgeable customers. They leave reps with little to do but compete on price. As we explored in our HBR article "The End of Solution Sales" (July–August 2012), the new environment favors creative and adaptable sellers who challenge customers with disruptive insights into their business—and offer unexpected solutions (see the sidebar "Selling to Empowered Customers").

Such "insight selling" is flexible, in recognition of the many possible routes to a sale. Delivering the right insight in the right way requires determining what the customer has already concluded about its needs and available solutions, who the decision makers are (often not the usual suspects), and what it will take to change their minds. The most effective approach to a sale varies, sometimes radically, from deal to deal. As a result, in recent years sales has seen a dramatic uncoupling of specific sales activities and specific outcomes; the sequential tactics that once led to predictable progress in a sale no longer do.

How can sales leaders best support insight selling? To find out, CEB spent the past year surveying 2,500 sales professionals from more than 30 B2B companies representing every major industry, geography, and go-to-market model in our client membership. We zeroed in on the managerial and organizational attributes most closely associated with star reps' success. And we corroborated quantitative findings through more than 100 structured interviews with heads of sales, sales operations, and sales excellence, and with frontline sales managers.

Idea in Brief

The Problem

The disciplined, process-oriented sales approach that has dominated for years is faltering. Sales cycle times are increasing, conversion rates are falling, margins are shrinking, and forecasts are becoming less reliable.

The Argument

Because customers are increasingly savvy about their needs and available solutions, sales reps must challenge them by offering disruptive insights and unexpected solutions. They can't accomplish that by adhering to strict processes.

The Lessons

Superior reps use their judgment and creativity to promote the customer behaviors that signal progress toward a sale. To support them, managers encourage collaborative strategy development and problem solving; communicate broadly and informally throughout the ranks; and focus on long-term rather than short-term performance.

The study showed that most large B2B organizations are still designed to achieve peak efficiency by ensuring that reps abide by an established "optimal" behavior. These organizations, all vivid examples of the sales machine, are marked by a strong process orientation, clear lines of authority, and close governance through formal rules. They particularly emphasize individual performance, nurturing a competitive atmosphere characterized by frequent contests, campaigns, and the regular updating of leaderboards. And they monitor sales reps through close attention to near-term metrics—especially cycle times and close rates.

When we look at the organizational climate most consistently associated with insight-selling behaviors, however, we find a mirror image of the sales machine, with two principal features: an organizational emphasis on the judgment of individual reps rather than their compliance with protocols; and a managerial focus on providing guidance and support rather than inspection and direction. Transforming a sales organization along those two dimensions is crucial for giving reps the support and latitude they need to win in the new environment.

Selling to Empowered Customers

SALES STRATEGY USED TO CENTER on answering a simple question: In a world where customers learn primarily from suppliers, how do you become the one that customers learn from first? Being that favored resource allowed suppliers to shape and ultimately win deals. The approach went like this: Identify customers early in their learning process; put a solution in front of them before anyone else does; highlight how it meets their needs; and push the deal through faster than competitors can.

Like their colleagues in manufacturing, sales leaders invested heavily in performance management systems designed to track how well reps complied with this process, and they continually tuned the performance of their sales machine. This approach worked well as long as suppliers offered discrete products and controlled the information about them.

But today, as suppliers have moved from selling individual, easily commoditized products to offering complex "solutions," customers—wary of the scale, disruption, and cost—have responded by scrutinizing deals more closely. They require consensus from more stakeholders than ever before; the days of the one-stop decision maker are over. IT sales executives complain that they must "sell beyond the CIO," and medical device suppliers grumble about the need to sell to purchasing organizations. Worse, even after they've tracked down these stakeholders and won them over, sales reps still need to stitch the buy-in of these individuals into an organizational decision.

Empowered customers now approach suppliers armed with a clear idea of their own needs, the potential solutions, and what they're willing to pay. When suppliers encounter such customers, there's often little left to negotiate but price.

As a result, a supplier's biggest competitive challenge today isn't so much the competition's ability to sell as it is the customer's ability to learn. Whereas competing against a rival's ability to sell requires superior sales discipline—more calls per hour, visits per week, and so on—competing against a customer's ability to learn requires superior teaching skills, a talent for revealing novel and important information about the business that the customer has overlooked. The best sales reps excel at this kind of teaching and can link the insights that arise to the solutions their firm provides.

The new world of sales

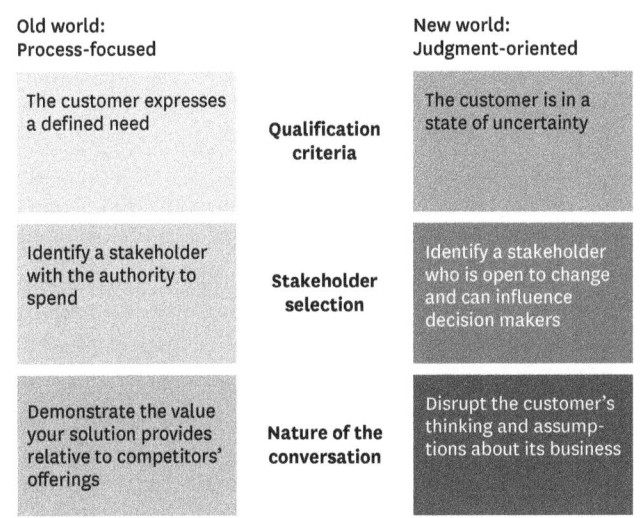

Changing the Organizational Climate

In a judgment-oriented sales organization, the climate is similar to what you'd find in other groups of highly skilled knowledge workers: Managers serve as coaches rather than as enforcers; the workforce self-manages to a large extent; the focus is on collaboration rather than competition; and the group is judged on long-term outcomes rather than short-term compliance with protocols.

To create this kind of environment, sales leaders must rethink how they manage and what they measure. Instead of demanding that a rep progress methodically through a checklist of sales activities, managers must focus on the customer's behaviors, especially any signals that the customer would be responsive to a new insight about its business. Such signals include acknowledging that the status quo isn't working, conceding that other suppliers' solutions are less viable, providing information typically not made available to other suppliers, and revising purchasing requirements and specifications in a way that reflects the supplier's advantages. This shift in focus gives reps greater latitude to use their judgment about the most-effective ways to drive a sale.

Our research points to a series of changes required to support a new organizational climate. First, our data reveal a strong emphasis in judgment-oriented sales organizations on creating demand early in the sales funnel rather than responding to it much later. This promotes pipeline building, not pipeline velocity. If compensation, dashboards, and sales campaigns all prioritize efficiency and speed, sales leaders unwittingly conspire with empowered customers to force their reps into the price-driven sale they were hoping to avoid. It's faster to close a deal with a customer that knows what it wants and is shopping for the lowest price than it is to challenge the customer's thinking and demonstrate that your solution offers the best value.

Second, the data highlight that managers in these organizations are giving reps greater latitude in the qualification, prioritization, and pursuit of individual opportunities. Our data do not suggest that process and structure are always bad. Nonetheless, reps are most likely to succeed in their interactions with empowered customers when they feel supported rather than directed, and when they are held accountable for outcomes rather than for performing certain activities. As one sales leader put it, "Today there's no 'single path to right,' only many paths to right that might equally be paths to wrong. So it's not the journey but the destination we have to focus on most."

Third, we observe a strong emphasis on encouraging innovation and a sense of business ownership among sales reps, with reps measured less on consistent execution of a one-size-fits-all approach and more on the overall profitable growth of their book of business.

These findings make many sales leaders nervous. The best reps will thrive in a judgment-oriented climate, but what about everyone else? Many average-performing reps benefit from—indeed, rely on—clear direction. It's important to note that providing the support those reps need doesn't mean returning to the sales machine approach. The key is to give them considerable discretion regarding their activities while guiding them through—and holding them accountable for—specific milestones on the way to a sale.

Let's look at two very different ways sales organizations today are creating a judgment-oriented climate. The first—a "customer-verified sales funnel"—is a well-known but infrequently applied approach rooted in the sales machine era. Traditionally in this model, salespeople and their managers have used a combination of rep activities and customer "verifiers," or behaviors, to track the progress of a deal. A simple example of a verifier is a customer's running a pilot application that a rep has suggested. Companies have tracked and measured such verifiers, but they have generally focused as much or more on the sales reps' actions leading up to the verifiers. Those actions are tracked in CRM systems, and the information is aggregated into a sales forecast or a pipeline review.

Leading sales organizations have embraced two important changes to this practice. First, they track and report only the customer verifiers, not the reps' actions. This change explicitly encourages reps to focus on achieving certain outcomes in the best way instead of simply executing activities in the prescribed way. As a result, reps are free to think more creatively about how to elicit certain reactions from individual customers. In a highly varied sales environment, specific activities may or may not be the best way. Second, the most advanced sales organizations are verifying not only the behaviors late in the process that indicate whether a customer is closer to making a purchase but also the behaviors very early in the process that signal whether the customer is ready and willing to change. This selling approach is about creating demand, not simply responding to it, so verifying whether the customer is ready to change is a prerequisite to pursuing a sale. Tracking this shift in customer attitude requires deeper scrutiny. For example, in addition to noting whether the customer has scheduled a demo, sellers look at whether a buying group has conceded that its existing approach is significantly underperforming.

Consider how the customer-verified sales funnel works at ADP, a global leader in human capital management. ADP identified a series of verifiers that reflect how its customers make a complex purchasing decision. Understanding these verifiers enabled sales managers to design better tools and provide better guidance to the sales force. Pipeline reviews, for example, have taken on a decidedly different tone. Instead of engaging in "spreadsheet coaching" ("Have you scheduled time with the decision makers?" "Did you determine whether they have a budget allocated for this purchase?" "Did you send our proposal?"), ADP managers collaborate with reps to think through how best to elicit specific customer verifiers. For example, if the verifier sought is "The customer agrees that the status quo is unsustainable," the manager might ask the rep, "How do we demonstrate to the customer that its current approach will expose it to substantial risk?" If the verifier is "The customer confirms that it has the budget to purchase our solution," the manager might ask, "How do we help the customer think creatively about funding if the money is not in this year's budget?" ADP sales reps, managers, and executives get in-depth exposure to this way of thinking during a three-day insight selling academy.

A leading global manufacturing firm we'll call Alpha Company takes a very different approach—one rarely seen in a large-scale field sales force—to creating a new sales climate. Alpha has assembled three-person "market teams"—each comprising an account executive, a solutions design specialist, and a project implementation manager—tasked with growing anywhere from 50 to 150 customers in a particular territory. Each team serves as a kind of franchise of the company, reporting directly to the region's general manager. Consequently, each team has full deal authority and P&L ownership to develop accounts however it sees fit, as long as the approach does not violate company policy. A team can follow a sales process or not. It can sell certain products and solutions or not. It's up to team members, collectively, to figure it all out. The only requirement is to turn in a profitable growth number for the territory. As at ADP, reps are accountable for the ends they achieve, not the means they use.

Alpha provides each team with a sales manager who functions not as a director but as a peer-level guide, helping to identify and implement innovative approaches to stalled deals (a rewrite of the manager's job we've never seen before). Although managers have the same objectives as the market teams they coach, the business holds the team accountable for delivering on them. Additionally, each team meets with a financial controller every two weeks to assess its strategy and review its likelihood of achieving growth.

After running the teams for a year now, the company has more than doubled its average deal size in these regions while reducing deal-level development costs by nearly 40%, and it is forecasting significantly higher revenue for the coming year. Moreover, sales reps from across the industry are now seeking employment with Alpha, attracted by its sales climate.

Changing What Managers Do

Our rep surveys revealed that despite the pressure to create a judgment-oriented sales climate, sales managers in most companies still seek compliance rather than judgment and creativity (see the exhibit "Compliance climates still dominate"). Nonetheless, a subset of managers—from companies such as Cargill, Oakwood Worldwide, Afton Chemical, Esri Australia, and Centurion Medical Products, to name a few—stand out for their ability to modify their local climates in order to encourage and support a new approach to selling. In interviews with them, we found that three behaviors separate them from the rest.

Facilitation

Rather than telling their teams what to do—or, as is common in sales, simply taking over deals—our exemplary sales managers serve as connectors within and beyond their teams, encouraging collaborative strategy development and problem solving. They live at the whiteboard, pulling team members into deal reviews and planning sessions. They encourage innovative thinking and push team members to challenge one another. As a result, reps on these teams know much more about activities in all territories than reps on other sales teams, and they commonly share ideas about how to handle an

Compliance climates still dominate

Sales reps need some latitude in how they engage highly knowledgeable and wary customers. But in many organizations—even those trying to adopt a new approach to selling—reps report that the sales climate is oriented toward monitoring their compliance with prescribed processes rather than encouraging them to exercise judgment.

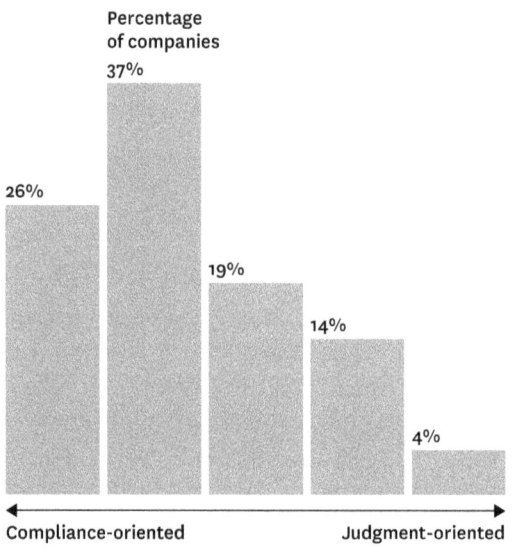

especially tricky deal or whether an opportunity is worth pursuing at all. One top manager, for example, made a point of having two new and two experienced sellers help tackle each challenge presented by a team member.

We've found from CEB's extensive research on employee productivity both within and beyond the sales function that one of the most important drivers is network performance: how effectively employees use their network of relationships to improve both their own and their peers' productivity. The exemplary sales managers we studied are experts at maximizing network performance within their teams;

Climate versus Culture

SOME SALES LEADERS WE SURVEYED expressed reservations about their ability to change the culture of their organizations in ways that would encourage reps to exercise judgment and creativity without changing the company-wide culture—a tall order.

But they were missing the important distinction, as our colleague William Macey has described it, between "culture" and "climate." Culture is made up of the deeply held beliefs and assumptions (sometimes unspoken) of a company's leaders and employees and is reinforced by outside stakeholders, including customers. It is hard for an individual leader to influence culture, because it arises from and is reinforced by tradition and history. Climate, as industrial and organizational psychologists describe it, is more pliable. It is a product not of implicit beliefs but of explicit organizational practices and activities. It reflects employees' experience of their day-to-day work environment. Leaders can create a new climate within sales through the signals they send, the priorities they set, and the operating environment of their teams.

---

they encourage team members to build, leverage, and contribute to their networks.

Informal communication

These managers regularly communicate up, down, and laterally. They provide a constant flow of information. As a result, they are intimately acquainted with their reps' territories, beyond what they read on a spreadsheet or hear in a pipeline review. Communication activities often happen outside structured settings, such as scheduled meetings. Likewise, managerial coaching isn't restricted to deal reviews and pipeline meetings, nor is it based on a rep's performance metrics in the latest dashboard. In fact, it's often transparent, occurring through a continual dialogue. These managers are constantly in teaching mode, listening to their teams, asking questions, and offering guidance. As one manager told us, "I don't have to force my team to compile call notes and deal reports, because we're always talking, even when my team is in the field. But I couldn't manage this way if they were all out there chasing bad business. To be this informal, every conversation has to be meaningful and move business forward."

Long-term focus

Rather than reward reps for short-term deal volume and velocity, these managers encourage them to cultivate business pipelines designed to generate substantial growth over the long term. It takes tremendous discipline to ignore the siren song of the close of each quarter, which leads reps to discount deals and sell simple products rather than complex solutions. Maintaining a focus on the long term requires managers to monitor customer verifiers, base sales forecasts on them, and direct reps' creativity and critical thinking to the most promising opportunities instead of overseeing processes and activities across a broad swath of potential deals.

A New Type of Talent

A judgment-oriented sales climate will divide the sales force, awakening the latent potential in many salespeople and leaving those who find reassurance in the directive world of the sales machine to struggle. As sales leaders recruit reps, they'll need to rethink their approach to ensure that the new hires will thrive in this climate.

Using data CEB collected on more than 4 million business professionals around the world, we found that only 17% of existing sales employees score high on the competencies required for success in insight selling. What's more, the sales labor market is skewed strongly toward emotional intelligence rather than IQ—reflecting a strong hiring bias in sales. But because sales today requires more judgment than ever before, the cognitive burden on the salesperson is significantly higher—emotional intelligence is not enough. In addition to using selection and assessment tools to identify the small percentage of salespeople who have a natural ability to succeed in this new climate, managers should consider hiring professionals not currently in sales roles who have excellent critical thinking skills and are willing to sell.

To attract and retain such nontraditional hires, leaders must overhaul their employment value proposition in two ways: First, they must emphasize the importance of collaboration and judgment. This talent demands an environment that supports individual

How reps use judgment

Here are some of the ways reps use judgment at each step in the sales process.

	STEPS IN THE PROCESS			
Cultivate the opportunity	Assess the customer's receptivity to insight	Challenge the customer's thinking	Build consensus	Close the deal
Determine if the opportunity is worth the investment of time	Make informed assumptions about the customer and its needs	Judge when best to engage key decision makers and other stakeholders	Tailor responses to stakeholders' highly varied objections and reactions	Assess the buying group's understanding of what differentiates the solution from the alternatives
Hypothesize about new ways to engage the customer	Identify atypical sources of information about the customer and its assumptions	Adapt the approach in order to generate buy-in	Creatively determine ways to revive stalled deals	Know when to stand firm or acquiesce in negotiation
Infer the scope of the opportunity on the basis of limited information about the customer	Exercise patience in order to allow an opportunity to develop	Assess the worthiness of the pursuit on the basis of the customer's reaction	Encourage and arm key stakeholders to influence detractors	Identify negotiation points beyond terms and conditions

decision making. To that end, as a practical measure, sales leaders would be well-advised to strike the following from virtually every sales job posting: "Wanted: experienced sales professionals looking to maximize earning potential in a fast-paced, competitive sales organization." Instead, they should position openings this way: "Wanted: critical thinkers looking for an opportunity to exercise their judgment and assume significant responsibility for business growth."

Second, they must shift the emphasis from extrinsic, short-term rewards such as heightened variable compensation to intrinsic, long-term motivators such as autonomy and the opportunity to generate value for customers. There's an old saying that "salespeople are coin-operated." But our data (and the work of others, including Daniel H. Pink in "A Radical Prescription for Sales," HBR July–August 2012) demonstrate that although short-term incentives are useful for driving simple, transactional sales, the effectiveness of these traditional pay structures diminishes as sales become more complex.

Our research shows that building a climate with the right incentives and rewards can boost the effort that salespeople make above and beyond their basic job requirements by 10% and increase their intent to stay by more than 30%.

The death of the sales machine is part of a much larger story—one that cuts across functions and industries and speaks to the changing nature of work. As the basis of economic growth shifts from transactional to knowledge work, management follows suit, turning its focus from building zero-error-rate manufacturing processes to recruiting and engaging high performers to drive innovation.

In sales, this shift is playing out before our eyes. The organizations that continue to embrace the sales machine model are watching margins fall as their solutions are commoditized and their best sales professionals seek different environments. As knowledge-work leaders know, the key to success, in the simplest terms, is to hire the best employees, create an empowering environment, provide the necessary tools and guidance, and then get out of the way.

Originally published in November 2013. Reprint R1311H

Tiebreaker Selling

by James C. Anderson, James A. Narus, and Marc Wouters

CUSTOMERS IN B2B MARKETS are becoming increasingly sophisticated about purchasing. Recognizing that most products and services they buy are not strategic to their businesses, they begin by simply seeking suppliers that will meet their basic specifications at a competitive price. Then, after they've winnowed down the contenders, they often ask the finalists to offer "something more."

Many suppliers misunderstand this request. They'll respond with the well-worn tactic of stressing features their offerings have but competitors' lack, and when that doesn't work, they propose price concessions. But it turns out that customers are looking for neither of those things.

During a three-year research project, we discovered that when purchasing managers ask for something more, they are actually looking for what we call *the justifier:* an element of an offering that would make *a noteworthy difference* to their company's business. A justifier's value to the customer is self-evident and provides a clearcut reason for selecting one supplier over others, effectively breaking the tie among the final contenders. A car-leasing company, for instance, might give customers the option to cancel a certain number of contracts prematurely without penalty. A construction company might offer to assign a client a senior project manager with whom it's had a successful experience, so the client would feel assured that the work wouldn't need to be audited and would be done on time and safely. A distributor of standard technical parts might put labels with the customer's own part numbers on packaging, eliminating the hassle and cost of translating the distributor's numbers to the customer's inventory system.

The justifier, or tiebreaker, helps the purchasing manager demonstrate to senior leadership that he or she is making a contribution to the business. That is no small thing. People responsible for nonstrategic purchases have difficult, often thankless, jobs. They're under pressure to complete these transactions as quickly and efficiently as possible. Whenever anything goes wrong with what they've bought, they get blamed. But their diligence and understanding of the business typically get little recognition.

To put it simply: Helping purchasing managers break out of this rut by giving them a visible "win" is how suppliers win. They gain a larger share of customers' business—and, potentially, the ability to price their offerings at or near the upper end of each customer's acceptable range.

Why Suppliers Misunderstand Customers

Strategic purchases are those that a business has decided contribute significantly to differentiating *its* offerings. Most purchases are not strategic. Nonetheless, nonstrategic purchases can be consequential, considering the large amount spent on them. Because companies need to make so many of them, the process for nonstrategic deals tends to be relatively simple, and the criteria for evaluating each decision are cursory: that it didn't consume too many resources and that there are no complaints or problems with the item selected.

We found that suppliers of nonstrategic products and services don't fully appreciate this purchasing task. So when they try to land a deal, they make two common mistakes.

They focus doggedly on their offerings' distinctive features even when customers don't want or need them.

The hope is that features that go beyond the specifications will win over the customer and get him or her to pay a premium. But trying to persuade a skeptical customer that such extras will add value is

Idea in Brief

The Problem

In B2B markets, suppliers of nonstrategic products and services assume they have only two options for landing sales: stressing features their offerings have but competitors' lack and competing on price.

The Research

A study of 46 companies found that this approach is ineffective, because customers often don't care much about the features touted and aren't seeking price concessions. Once they have narrowed the competition down to finalists that meet basic specifications and are within an acceptable price range, customers instead are looking for "something more."

The Solution

Taking the time to understand the customer's business and priorities in order to identify the tiebreaking justifier—a noteworthy extra whose value is self-evident and will enhance the standing of purchasing managers in their organizations—will seal the deal more effectively.

---

no easy task, as a story we heard from the director of supply management at a U.S. teaching hospital shows. She related to us how the salesperson for a supplier that had developed an antimicrobial coating for its sutures always pitched her that premium-priced product, even though ordinary sutures are fine for most surgical applications.

They offer price concessions that customers don't want.
During initial requests for quotes for nonstrategic offerings, purchasing managers vet potential suppliers on basic requirements and price. As long as suppliers meet the former and their price quotes fall within a reasonable range—plus or minus 3% to 5% of the other finalists' prices is common—the purchasers let them stay in the competition and then ask them what else they can offer. Many suppliers' reflex reaction is to lower the price.

But this move can actually create more work for purchasing managers. They often have to go back to the other finalists and offer them a chance to cut their prices too, to get the prices back within an acceptable range of one another. And after happily taking any price reductions, the purchasing manager again raises the request for "something more," which isn't surprising. If the only goal was to obtain the lowest possible price, why would the business need the purchasing manager? Reverse electronic auctions could perform the job.

We discovered that even when the other finalist suppliers won't reduce their prices, purchasing managers frequently are still reluctant to choose the lowest bid, fearing that it's too good to be true. An executive in the construction industry told us that he worries such suppliers are trying to buy the business or do not fully understand their cost structures. In either case, they may do one of two things if they win the deal: try to recoup the concession further down the road by charging stiff penalties for any changes, or cut corners and compromise on quality.

Why do suppliers fall back on these ineffective practices rather than proposing justifiers? Many myopically conclude that since their basic offerings are more or less the same as those of competitors, it doesn't pay to invest resources in selling them, and it's better to focus on managing costs. That mentality leads suppliers to pressure their salespeople to get what business they can without delay, causing them to cut short the time they spend with most customers. As a result, salespeople sometimes ignore direct customer requests that can easily lead to justifiers.

At times the purchasing manager will prefer to do business with one of the finalists and, rather than sharing a concern with all of them, will relate it just to that one firm. If the salesperson takes the time to listen and devise a solution, the purchasing manager has his or her justifier and can then make the deal and move on to other business.

This was the situation with the food safety division of a leading pest-prevention company, which equipped its technicians with PC tablets that helped them follow service protocols and generate invoices. The company was looking to replace the devices, which were on several different leases. A thorny issue was that during the transition period, as old leases were phased out and a new one went into effect, the division would have to make double lease payments, which would adversely affect its bottom line for three months and, as a result, operations managers' bonuses.

The purchasing manager was leaning toward one of the equipment leasing companies on his shortlist, which had an especially good business relationship with the equipment provider. So he asked its sales rep: "What can we do to get rid of this overlap and the double lease payments?" The supplier offered to defer payment on the new leases for the replacement tablets for three months by consolidating the 36 monthly payments into 33. While the company would actually pay the same total amount for the tablets, it wouldn't get hit with two sets of bills at once, and the operations managers would get their bonuses. The purchasing manager told us that if this leasing company had not offered such a solution, he would have taken a harder look at the other finalists.

How to Discover Justifiers

We studied 46 companies located in the United States and Europe, which operated in a variety of industries, including beverages, construction materials, facilities maintenance, health care, logistics and transportation, power generation, and staffing services. To get the customer perspective, we interviewed the top executives, supply chain directors, and purchasing managers at 31 companies, and to get the supplier perspective, the top managers, salespeople, and marketing and business-development executives at 15 companies.

From this research we learned that exceptional suppliers—or tiebreaking sellers—invest resources in a process for finding, vetting, and developing justifiers. They investigate three potential sources of ideas for justifiers:

How customers actually use the offering

Tiebreaking sellers coach their salespeople to explore this topic with customers and engage them in a conversation about their concerns. Consider Gerdau Long Steel North America, a leading supplier of rebar, the steel rods used to reinforce concrete. Rebar might seem like the ultimate commodity product—one that's difficult to differentiate and can be sold only on the basis of price. But Gerdau has found that this is not the case.

Rebar is cut into 60-foot lengths, put into bundles of one to five tons, and strapped together at four or five different points. If the rebar rods lie flat when the bundles are opened, it's easier to feed them into a shearer or bender, where they're cut to specified lengths and fabricated into concrete reinforcements. But often the rods arrive intertwined, so a worker has to shake each one to get it to lie flat, which slows processing and adds to customers' costs.

Gerdau learned of this issue in a quarterly business review with one of its large customers. Many customers rate their suppliers and share the ratings with them at such reviews. At Gerdau the salesperson and regional sales manager usually conduct this meeting with the customer, but depending on the agenda, Gerdau senior management or experts in domains like metallurgy, logistics, and operations also may participate.

Gerdau's salespeople have been taught to use the reviews to start a dialogue: Which ratings would the customer most want Gerdau to improve? What exactly is meant by particular ratings such as "ease of doing business"? How could Gerdau raise its ratings?

The sales personnel also make it a point to ask an open-ended question at the end of each review: "How can we be a better supplier to you?" That encourages the customer's managers to respond in an expansive fashion and bring up something they might otherwise neglect. It was this question, in fact, that prompted the large customer to mention rebar intertwining.

That concern was relayed to senior sales management at Gerdau's monthly sales meetings, where potential fixes for one-off issues are discussed and implemented. It was then taken up at Gerdau's monthly improvement meeting, where senior management and domain experts examine more-complex issues and investigate new ways to deliver value to customers. Soon Gerdau figured out the cause of the intertwining: After a rod was cut to length, it would fall two to four feet, which imparted mechanical energy to it and created a whipsaw effect. The company then revamped its production process to prevent this from happening.

The lie-flat rods lower the cost of fabricating and placing rebar by around 25%, Gerdau determined. The competitive advantage

Value selling versus tiebreaker selling

With value selling, suppliers build a case to prove that their offerings provide greater worth to customers than competitors' do. But when purchases aren't strategic, that approach is ineffective, and suppliers need something extra whose value is self-evident to win the sale.

	Value selling	Tiebreaker selling
Supplier's core offering	Highly differentiated The product or service has unique features that customers appreciate	Undifferentiated The customers want only their basic specs met at a competitive price
Customer's view of the purchase	Strategic The purchase significantly contributes to differentiating the customer's offerings	Not strategic The purchase is not critical to differentiating the customer's offerings
Customer's willingness to extensively evaluate the offering's value	High	Low
Deal winner	Quantified value of offering The offering provides quantifiably higher value than that of competing offerings, which more than compensates for its higher price	A "justifier" The supplier offers an extra that the customer finds valuable without analysis and that shows the purchasing manager's contribution to the business
Supplier's goal	A significant price premium (>5%)	A slight price premium (3%–5%)

is intuitive to customers, but by sharing these savings estimates Gerdau enables purchasing managers to better show their senior managers that they are helping reduce costs.

Randstad, a provider of temporary staffing and other HR services, takes a different approach to exploring how customers use its offerings. In addition to having its account managers probe customers' purchasing and human resources departments, Randstad sends its process managers, who are experts in staffing practices and industry and regional trends, to talk with operations managers at customers' sites. The process managers use a questionnaire that starts broadly with queries about what kind of lead times and flexibility the customer's customers expect. Next, it zooms in on the customer's own operations and delves into details such as which activities require flexible staffing and what skills are needed to perform those activities. That helps the process managers identify a likely justifier for each customer, like assistance in determining how workers could be shared across departments.

Opportunities to integrate offerings with those of other companies

Suppliers should explore how their products and services relate to other purchases the customer is making and how they might be combined to provide added value. This was an approach taken by a supplier of GPS devices to the pest-prevention outfit mentioned earlier. The GPS company often found itself in deals that involved purchases from complementary suppliers and took the initiative in reaching out to them.

It won the pest-prevention firm's business by proposing that it integrate its data on driver behavior (for example, on accelerating or braking too fast and excessive idling) with the data of the companies that maintained the pest-prevention firm's fleet and supplied the payment cards the drivers used to buy fuel. The resulting reports allowed the pest-prevention firm to better manage its vehicle maintenance costs and to determine when fuel purchased on its cards was being pumped into unauthorized vehicles.

The customers' business priorities

The top yearly goals of a customer's senior management can be a great source of ideas for justifiers. By visiting a customer's website or perusing its annual report, a supplier can learn about initiatives aimed at improving safety in specific areas, reducing waste, and the like. Yet purchasing managers told us that salespeople rarely conduct such rudimentary background research or put in the time to learn about their customers' objectives.

That's an oversight, because a little exploration can go a long way. A packaging company that sells to Bayer CropScience, a provider of seeds, crop protection, and nonagricultural pest control, asked two questions at the end of the Bayer purchasing manager's quarterly review of its performance: "What's important to you?" and "What do your customers need?" The aim of the first was to identify the corporate objectives that mattered most to the purchasing manager. The aim of the second was to understand the goals that Bayer was trying to help its customers achieve. The packaging company learned that Bayer had made lowering all inventory- and logistics-related costs a priority and that a number of its customers were trying to make progress on sustainability. So when the purchasing manager asked for "something more," the vendor came back with an offer to share its design and engineering capabilities to help Bayer revamp its packaging—something Bayer lacked the expertise to do on its own.

The new packaging was lighter and required less secondary packaging, which aligned Bayer with its customers' sustainability initiatives. It also let Bayer put more products on a pallet, allowing it to fit more products in each truck and stack them higher in warehouses. It provided a win for the purchasing manager, who was being evaluated on the logistics savings he could help generate.

Creating New Businesses

Sometimes the search for a justifier can lead to a new source of revenue and profit. A service that North Carolina-based TLC Van/Pickup Upfitters offers illustrates how.

The company designs and installs shelving, equipment racks, and other functional items in commercial vans. Most of its competitors consider their job done once they have completed an installation. Not TLC. After an installation, it will inspect customers' vans twice a year at their locations at no charge. If the customer desires, TLC will then do whatever maintenance is needed—tighten loose bolts, fix shelving that is coming off the walls, repair drawers that aren't working—at a reasonable price.

This can save customers lots of money: If not addressed early on, a minor problem that TLC would charge $30 to fix can become a $1,000 repair and take a van out of service. In addition to saving fleet managers time and hassle, TLC provides them with a win: It gives them concrete examples of the cost savings that timely repairs deliver, which the fleet managers can pass along to their senior managers.

TLC spotted this justifier a few years ago, when it helped a large customer solve a problem with ladder racks. It learned that many technicians driving the vans didn't believe it was their responsibility to maintain the fittings and often didn't tell fleet managers about emerging maintenance issues.

Performing the inspections has allowed TLC to position itself as a preferred supplier and earn more of its customers' business. And the preventive maintenance service has become an integral part of the company's offerings: Three years after it was launched, it accounted for 15% of TLC's revenues.

Identifying Fresh Justifiers

By their nature, successful justifiers have a limited life span. Customers' priorities and concerns change, and competitors catch on and match your moves. This means that a supplier has to be on the continual lookout for fresh justifiers.

The exemplary suppliers we studied approach that task with a structured process. Take UPS. Understanding the ongoing need to find segment-specific justifiers, the logistics and transportation-services firm has reorganized its marketing and selling efforts around targeted industry segments such as health care, retail, and professional services, as well as U.S. regions with strong growth potential. Each segment and region has its own marketing and sales managers who reside in the field.

In the past, ideas for new services and justifiers came mainly from UPS's new-product development unit in Atlanta and often took a long time to implement. Today, UPS encourages its segment and regional marketing and sales managers to offer ideas at periodic meetings. In addition to an annual meeting in Atlanta, which they all attend, UPS holds two monthly teleconferences, one at the regional level and a second at the national level. Both conference calls have lots of structured brainstorming. The calls begin with postmortems of recent deals that UPS either won or lost. Participants then bring up new business challenges customers face and explore gaps between UPS's current offerings and emerging customer requirements, as well as any competitor efforts to address the gaps. The meetings conclude by proposing new services and justifiers that might effectively and profitably plug the gaps.

One new justifier that emerged from the meetings was Customized Express Envelopes. During a regional conference call, a marketing manager noted that while a key requirement of professional services is brand building, few small and midsize firms have enough resources to do it. He then made a breakthrough observation: Those firms used a lot of overnight express envelopes, and those envelopes were largely blank. He proposed that UPS print the customer's logo or advertisement on them. During that call and the subsequent national one, participants fine-tuned the idea and examined its costs. Several account representatives then pitched it to customers informally and found that it resonated. After a pilot test yielded a reasonable increase in sales and profits, UPS introduced Customized Express Envelopes. UPS managers report that the envelopes have enabled them to win significant new business in the small to midsize company segment.

Most suppliers of nonstrategic products and services think they have few options other than selling on price or pushing distinctive features that don't really matter to customers. In the vast majority of cases, these suppliers are wasting their time and resources. The justifier approach is an attractive alternative.

But like any major change, it won't come easily. It requires investments in new structures and processes. And more often than not, it means suppliers will have to change the established mind-set of their executives and salespeople. But the successes with the approach that we discovered demonstrate that with enough determination, even a supplier of a nonstrategic offering can persuade its customers' purchasing managers and leadership that it is something special.

Originally published in March 2014. Reprint R1403G

Making the Consensus Sale

by Karl Schmidt, Brent Adamson, and Anna Bird

SALES REPS HAVE LONG BEEN taught to seek out the executive who can single-handedly approve a deal at a company. But whether they're selling to a customer with 50 employees or 50,000, reps today rarely find a unilateral decision maker. More often, they discover that the authority to make decisions rests with groups of individuals—all of whom have different roles, and all of whom have veto power. Reaching consensus and closing deals has become an increasingly painful and protracted process for customers and suppliers alike.

To understand the impact of buying groups on sales, CEB recently conducted four surveys of more than 5,000 stakeholders involved in B2B purchases. We found that, on average, 5.4 people now have to formally sign off on each purchase. Complicating matters, the variety of jobs, functions, and geographies that these individuals represent is much wider than it used to be. Whereas an IT supplier might have once sold directly to a CIO and his or her team, today that same firm may also need buy-in from the chief marketing officer, the chief operating officer, the chief financial officer, legal counsel, procurement executives, and others. The people on buying teams have increasingly diverse priorities, and to win them over, suppliers must bridge those differences. The upshot is longer cycle times, smaller deals, lower margins, and, in the ever more common worst case, customer deadlock that scuttles the deal. (See the exhibit "Group size matters.")

Innovative suppliers, however, are finding effective ways to create consensus in these buying groups. This article describes how those companies prime groups with a common language and shared perspectives, motivate internal champions to advocate for their firms' solutions, and equip those champions to help groups reach agreement. As we'll see, accomplishing all of this requires some novel approaches and a new level of collaboration between sales and marketing.

Understanding Customer Consensus

CEB's surveys spanned a wide range of industries, geographies, and go-to-market models and an even larger array of issues associated with group purchases—everything from buying-group demographics to purchase-process dynamics to individual behavior. Three key conclusions emerged from the responses:

1. Personalization can backfire.

Conventional wisdom holds that the more personalized a message is, the more effectively it will drive a sale. And indeed, CEB's surveys found that individual customer stakeholders who perceived supplier content to be tailored to their specific needs were 40% more willing to buy from that supplier than stakeholders who didn't. Marketers understand this: In another survey, 95% of nearly 200 B2B CMOs identified "better tailoring of content" as a top priority. But personalization has a dark side. When individuals in a buying group receive different messages, each one stressing that an offering meets his or her narrow needs, it can highlight the diverging goals and priorities in the group, driving a wedge between members and hindering consensus.

The implication for suppliers is clear: The best way to build customer consensus isn't to do a better job of connecting individual customer stakeholders to the supplier but to more effectively connect customer stakeholders to one another.

Idea in Brief

The Problem

Increasingly, decisions about large company purchases are made not by individual executives but by a group of managers. Because group members often have different priorities, getting them to reach agreement poses a big challenge for suppliers.

The Solution

Salespeople must learn to build consensus. They can do so by helping buying-group members discover shared language and goals; motivating individual members of the group to become advocates for their firms' solutions; and equipping those advocates to teach and persuade.

The Benefits

Consensus building taps capabilities within both sales and marketing. Companies that encourage the two functions to collaborate on consensus-focused strategies are seeing decisive improvements in sales performance.

2. Achieving consensus is hardest early in the buying process.
To help groups reach decisions, it's critical to understand where in the purchase process they run into trouble. Our research divided the typical process into three phases: problem definition, solution identification, and supplier selection. We then asked customer stakeholders to look at both group and individual decisions and say which phases of them were most difficult.

Two results stood out: B2B buyers found group decision making most difficult twice as often as individual decision making. More important, the phase they seemed to experience the most challenges with was identifying a solution—agreeing on the best course regardless of supplier. Most suppliers are focusing on the wrong stage of the buying process, falling all over themselves to persuade customers to choose them, rather than helping customers settle on a solution.

Our data shows that customers are, on average, 37% of the way through a purchase process by the time they reach the solution-definition stage, and 57% of the way through the process before they engage with supplier sales reps. So all too often customer consensus has fallen apart before reps even arrive on the scene. If suppliers aren't anticipating and proactively overcoming disconnections

Group size matters

The likelihood of a purchase drops sharply as the number of decision makers increases.

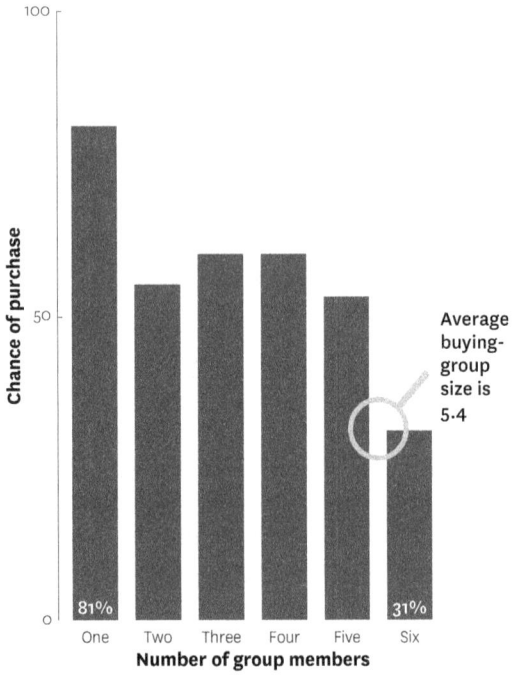

Source: CEB/Motista 2013 B2B brand survey

among stakeholders before sales engagements, they're probably losing many deals—without even knowing it.

Achieving customer consensus presents not just a problem for sales but also an opportunity for marketing. Marketing departments are well positioned to foster consensus for two reasons: They have tools that can reach customers more effectively than sales can during the critical consensus-building process, and they can combine customer knowledge from sales with their own market research to identify patterns of customer behavior and broad customer insights that they can translate into scalable marketing approaches and materials.

3. Willingness to buy and willingness to advocate are not the same.

Because a supplier has limited access to buying-group members during the early stages of the process, it needs the active help of an advocate inside the customer organization. We call these people "mobilizers." Mobilizers come in many forms, but the best are motivated to improve their organization; are passionate about sharing their insights with colleagues; ask smart, probing questions; and have the organizational clout and connections to bring decision makers together.

But to effectively use mobilizers, suppliers must address two challenges: the willingness of individuals to advocate on a supplier's behalf, and their ability to do so. A CEB survey of nearly 600 B2B buyers found that fully half the people who reported a willingness to buy a product or service were not willing to publicly advocate for it. This represents a huge obstacle for suppliers seeking to leverage mobilizers to create consensus.

Research shows that potential mobilizers are inhibited by the perceived risks inherent in fighting for change and promoting consensus. Up to half fear losing respect or credibility in their organization if they push for an unpopular purchase or are unable to attract support, or if the purchase they backed turns out to be unwise. Twelve percent even report that such advocacy could threaten their jobs. (The old saying "Nobody ever got fired for buying IBM" speaks to this point; potential advocates don't want to be the person who went out on a limb for the "wrong" supplier.) Fear of these consequences increases dramatically as the size of a buying team grows.

Ultimately, the decision to publicly advocate for change is driven much more by the personal value provided to the mobilizer than by the business value provided to that individual's organization. In studying what inspires mobilizers, we found that factors such as whether a solution could advance a person's career or help him be seen as a better leader were five times as potent as the offering's "business value"—things like superior product features, likely impact on business outcomes, or return on investment.

Overcoming potential mobilizers' perceptions of personal risk requires a personal appeal, not just an organizational one. This is a deeply telling point, because the most common tools in suppliers' tool kits—for example, ROI calculators, lifetime-value assessments, and total-cost-of-ownership scorecards—address organizational risks and rewards but say very little about individual ones. Once again, suppliers are emphasizing the wrong things with their sales and marketing investments.

But even when someone sees the personal value to be gained and is motivated to become a mobilizer, he or she will need support. Marketing has a key role to play in both encouraging mobilizers and equipping them to build consensus.

Creating Customer Consensus

In research with hundreds of organizations and thousands of sales and marketing executives, we have identified three strategies that are key in building consensus. Below, we'll describe each of them in detail, illustrating them with selected examples of approaches that have proved effective at the companies that belong to CEB Marketing.

1. Priming customer buying groups for agreement by creating a common language and shared perspectives around a problem and a solution

The starting point in any program to build consensus is to identify common ground among stakeholders. If you're selling enterprise marketing-management solutions, you'll most likely be dealing with at least the CMO, the CIO, the CFO, and procurement, who all have overlapping but distinct and sometimes conflicting interests. Helping those stakeholders see their shared interests will set the stage for consensus and make it easier—and less risky—for mobilizers to advocate on your behalf.

Two approaches can help purchase decision makers focus on what unites rather than what separates them:

Language mapping. Like many companies, the network and security solutions provider Cisco mines social media and online publications to track trending terms and themes in its space. By analyzing the phrases surrounding terms of interest, Cisco captures the context of online conversations and can identify the priorities of various stakeholders as well as topics that might appeal to them. For example, in discussions of smart devices, it found that both CMOs and CIOs focused on "connectivity," though the CMOs might refer a lot to "product development" and "innovation," and CIOs to "systems upgrades" and "network architecture."

The area of overlap—"connectivity"—gave Cisco's marketers the raw materials to develop messaging. They crafted a range of experimental messages (such as "connectivity isn't as high as you think" and "Only 1% of devices are connected so far"), embedded them in social media, and then tracked adoption of the language in online conversations among both stakeholder groups. The marketing team then integrated resonating concepts and tested messages into collateral, such as tweets, blogs, and white papers, to help create a common language and shared perspectives among stakeholders. Cisco's sales reps report that this approach has raised interest in connectivity—which Cisco's products enable—among both CIOs and CMOs, increasing alignment between two often disconnected parties.

Shared learning. In some cases stakeholders believe that no common ground exists and that their interests are mutually exclusive. A production manager, for example, may feel that her goals for efficiency are deeply different from a safety officer's goals—though in fact they aren't. In such cases, shared learning experiences can expose common priorities.

Kimberly-Clark Professional (KCP) sells health and safety products and services to businesses worldwide. To make enterprise sales such as airframe maintenance solutions, KCP may have to align the seemingly diverse interests of production managers, safety officers, sustainability heads, purchasing managers, and others who need to agree on a purchase. One way KCP achieves this is through facilities assessments, or site surveys, that provide shared learning. Marketing promotes the surveys on its website and sends potential customers invitations explaining the benefits of "learning tours" in which KCP experts visit facilities, offer advice on improvements, and answer questions. Typically, the accompanying materials promise guidance on how to control costs, increase productivity, reduce workers' exposure to hazardous materials, and increase environmental performance—highlighting the stakeholders' shared needs. After the walk-through, KCP provides a report summarizing its findings and recommendations.

Greif, a global industrial packaging manufacturer, takes another approach to shared learning. Companies in its industry generally struggle with commoditization, as most purchasing decisions are based solely on cost. Realizing that connecting offerings with customers' sustainability goals could elevate packaging decisions to a more strategic level, Greif developed a diagnostic tool that potential customers can use to evaluate the environmental benefits of various operational changes, including switching to lightweight shipping containers. The calculator (called the Green Tool) requires the participation of multiple stakeholders and, like the KCP learning tours, helps decision makers with different goals discover their areas of alignment. A sustainability head, for example, understanding that a packaging switch could reduce the firm's CO_2 emissions, might reach out to purchasing and plant managers for data the tool requires—such as container weights and volume, transport distances, and trippage rates (a measure of a reusable container's life span)—to calculate the emissions impact of various containers over their life cycles. The Green Tool reveals cost and sustainability benefits that resonate for each stakeholder—not just the sustainability head—moving the group toward a shared decision to purchase. In the three years following the introduction of the tool, sales of Greif's sustainable products and services have increased significantly. For example, sales of lightweight plastic drums grew by about 15% from 2011 to 2013.

Converting Sales Tools into Mobilizer Tools

SUPPLIERS OFTEN HAVE SALES collateral that could be repurposed to help internal champions, or "Mobilizers," build consensus around purchases within customers' organizations. When adapting those materials, marketers should follow these three principles:

1. Make content supplier neutral. Mobilizers will reject anything that makes them look like shills. To be credible, information on both the problem and the solution should not promote any one supplier or offering, though it's OK to clarify elements of the problem or the solution that your company is uniquely able to address.

2. Minimize mobilizers' efforts. Mobilizers will act only if they feel that the personal value of promoting a product or service outweighs the effort of doing so. Ensure that the recommendations in materials are as clear and simple to execute as possible. Remove technical language, streamline processes, and clarify how much time and information will be required to tailor materials to the mobilizers' organizations.

3. Address knowledge or skill gaps. Mobilizers don't have the benefit of your sales reps' experience. Leverage any existing materials that document your reps' expertise, such as purchase-process knowledge, cross-functional perspectives, or persuasive tactics. Where necessary, create new tools by partnering with sales to understand common obstacles and easy ways around them.

2. Motivating mobilizers

As discussed, your potential mobilizers may fear they'll hurt their credibility and job security by lobbying for a specific solution. They must believe the rewards of advocacy will outweigh the risk and effort. There are two important levers marketers can use to shift the risk/reward balance in the right direction.

Decrease individuals' perceived risk. Potential mobilizers often hesitate to recommend a purchase because they're unsure that others in the organization will support their position. The results of one of our surveys—of 3,000 employees across a range of organizations—hammered home that point: Willingness to advocate for a purchase more than doubled as perceived organizational support for a supplier increased. The challenge for suppliers, then, is to reveal this support. The shared learning events described earlier can help, but more-focused approaches that target individual advocates and encourage them to speak up are critical to getting the customer group to participate in such events or engage with diagnostic tools in the first place.

Holcim, a global supplier of cement and related products and services for the construction industry, uses a simple and effective tactic to do this. As a component of its sales operations, Holcim regularly surveys people throughout its customers' organizations to collect Net Promoter Scores (which gauge willingness to recommend a product or a company). If an account manager encounters a potential advocate for a new offering at an existing customer, a Holcim rep can present that person with NPS data from other functions that demonstrates broad support for Holcim's offerings. Reps report that advocates are often unaware of allies within their organization until they see the NPS numbers and say that the data gives those allies confidence to promote a purchase.

Increase perceived rewards. Connecting with customers' emotions has long been central to consumer marketing. It's less common in the B2B world, where sales and marketing typically focus on conveying the business value of products and services. But combining perceived value with an emotional tie can make all the difference in motivating a mobilizer.

W.W. Grainger, a global provider of maintenance, repair, and operations (MRO) solutions, traditionally sold to facility managers who had wide latitude in selecting MRO suppliers. But with pressure to contain costs growing, facility managers were increasingly required to defend their choices. Grainger started finding that many weren't motivated to make a case for using Grainger, despite its premium offerings, as other suppliers were often perceived as "good enough."

Through its market research, Grainger discovered that facility managers see themselves as behind-the-scenes problem solvers who face daily obstacles to keeping their plants running safely and efficiently. Out of this finding came "Get It. Got It. Good," a campaign designed to demonstrate a direct connection between Grainger's unique capabilities and managers' desire to run facilities at peak performance. The campaign reflected the gritty reality of the job and conveyed that Grainger understood the challenges facility managers face and their fear of missteps that would cause downtime.

The result of the campaign? Reps report that facility managers feel that Grainger "gets them" better than competitors do and are more motivated to advocate for Grainger products. The campaign has dramatically outperformed expectations, delivering 175% of expected returns.

3. Equipping mobilizers to be effective

Mobilizers typically aren't salespeople. They usually aren't experienced with change processes, may lack a cross-functional perspective, and may not be skilled at persuasion. Suppliers can help them in all these areas. Indeed, 80% of the mobilizers we surveyed told us they wanted support from suppliers in communicating the value of solutions they championed.

In an earlier time, providing that support would have principally been a sales task. But because the challenges to achieving consensus often emerge before sales has a foot in the door, this task increasingly falls to marketing. Progressive marketing teams, we've found, are adeptly converting sales-enablement materials to support mobilizers, making those materials freely available early in the consensus process, and distributing them in lead-nurturing e-mails, through blogs, and in myriad other ways.

Consider one approach used by Marketo, a provider of marketing automation software. Marketo created a 100-page mobilizer tool kit, "The Definitive Guide to Marketing Automation," which it e-mails to leads and posts on its website. The tool kit covers everything from what marketing automation is to the future of the technology. But its central chapters zero in on the specifics mobilizers need to make their business case internally. It provides detailed guidance on how to communicate the value of marketing automation to diverse stakeholders, including the CEO, the CMO, the CFO, the CIO, and the head of sales, walking readers through the chief concerns of each executive and how to address them. It also offers tips on the art of persuasion, including the need to understand management's objectives and to create a financial case, and the importance of "discussing, not presenting." The arguments given are supported with case studies. Finally, the guide takes mobilizers through the purchase process, with a primer on aligning internal stakeholders and selecting a vendor. While the guide carries the Marketo brand, it is conspicuously supplier agnostic, devoting only a single page, tucked at the end, to Marketo's solution.

CEB has presented the Marketo case to hundreds of marketing executives in dozens of sessions. In every session at least one CMO says he or she has already used Marketo's tool kit in purchasing marketing automation software. Pam Boiros, vice president of corporate marketing at Skillsoft, found the concept so compelling that she decided to create a similar tool for Skillsoft. Says Boiros, "Many of our sales team members tell us they are using this guide—in whole or in part—to set expectations with customers, help guide the purchase decision, and influence RFPs."

The biggest change in sales and marketing today is how customers buy. The new need to create consensus is turning decades of conventional sales wisdom on its head—replacing the requirement that sales focus first on connecting the customer with the supplier with a requirement to connect decision makers within a customer's organization with one another. The other major requirement, more implicit than explicit in this article, is that the relationship between sales and marketing finally change. Companies have long paid lip service to the need for sales and marketing to play together nicely. But given today's pressure to drive consensus, suppliers that don't align sales and marketing as a single team with a common goal will be trounced by suppliers that do.

Originally published in March 2015. R1503H

The Right Way to Use Compensation

by Mark Roberge

I WAS THE FOURTH EMPLOYEE hired at HubSpot. I'd met the two cofounders when we were all pursuing graduate degrees at MIT's Sloan School of Management. They're smart guys with a big mission: to help companies transform their marketing by using online content to draw potential customers to their websites—a practice known as "inbound" marketing.

My job was to build the sales team. An engineer by training, I'd never worked in sales—I'd begun my career writing code. But my background proved to be more of an advantage than I'd expected. It led me to challenge many conventional notions of sales management, using the metrics-driven, process-oriented lens through which I'd been trained to see the world. For instance, instead of hiring by instinct, I meticulously tracked data on sales, identified predictors of success, and looked for people whose traits and skills closely resembled those of our top sellers. Instead of training new recruits by having them tag along on a successful salesperson's calls, I created a regimented training program that gave them firsthand experience with our technology and then taught them to systematically work leads.

That approach worked well: Within seven years of its founding, HubSpot crossed the $100 million run-rate revenue mark and had acquired more than 10,000 customers in over 60 countries. In the fall of 2014 our company went public in an offering worth $125 million.

When I look back on the various strategies I used to grow our sales force from zero to several hundred people, I realize that one of the biggest lessons I've learned involves the power of a compensation plan to motivate salespeople not only to sell more but to act in ways that support a start-up's evolving business model and overall strategy.

Whether you're a CEO or a VP of sales, the sales compensation plan is probably the most powerful tool you have. Most of the critical strategic shifts that HubSpot made as a business were executed through changes to the sales compensation plan. In this article I will look at how we did this and at the general principles you should keep in mind when designing your own firm's plan.

Knowing What You Need and When

Business leaders often ask, "What's the best sales compensation structure to use?" It's a complicated question. The ideal plan is contextual—tailored to both the type of business and the stage of growth the company is in. Start-ups typically go through three key stages: customer acquisition, customer retention and success, and sustainable growth. In the first seven years at HubSpot, we used three different sales compensation plans, each of which was appropriate for the stage our business was in at the time.

1. The customer acquisition plan

HubSpot's first compensation plan was oriented toward "hunting" new customers. When we put it in place, we had 100 customers and an annual run rate of barely $300,000. Like most start-ups at this stage of development, we needed to acquire customers quickly so that we could see how valuable our offering actually was to them. We'd been pretty good at gathering feedback from potential customers as we'd developed our product—which is true of most new ventures—but the real test would be asking customers for money.

The first plan paid salespeople a base salary and $2 up front for every $1 of monthly recurring revenue they brought in. To protect the company if customers defected, we implemented a four-month

Idea in Brief

The Challenge

A start-up often changes direction as it grows. As the strategy shifts, it's critical that the employees who bring in the revenue—the sales force—understand and behave in ways that support the new strategy. The sales compensation system can help ventures achieve that alignment.

The Prescription

Revise the incentive system to focus salespeople on new goals at each growth phase. The start-up HubSpot did this; it implemented a plan that encouraged rapid customer acquisition early on, but switched to a second plan to promote customer retention and then to a third geared for sustainable growth.

The Result

Changes to the sales compensation plan helped HubSpot quickly grow its business to $100 million in annual revenue and acquire more than 10,000 customers in 60 countries.

---

clawback on commissions. This meant that if a customer jumped ship within the first four months, HubSpot took the entire commission back (deducting it from the salesperson's earned commissions the next month). Once a customer had stayed on the platform for four months, the salesperson could keep the entire commission even if the customer later canceled.

This plan was simple, clean, and hunting oriented. It worked well to accelerate the pace of new customer acquisition. In under six months our base shot up to 1,000 customers, and our revenue hit $3 million.

2. The customer success and retention plan

With plenty of customers on board, we could now analyze how well the company was progressing toward "product/market fit"—the point at which product features and pricing are aligned with the market's preferences. The biggest sign that the fit wasn't perfect was a clear problem with customer retention. Among our early customers, the level of churn was unsustainable. This was not surprising. It's rare that a start-up finds a fit on its first attempt with customers. That's why a fast feedback cycle, proper diagnosis of the issues, and quick, disciplined iteration are necessary during this stage. At this point in a start-up's evolution, it's key to figure out who your best customers are and what steps will make them successful.

Looking for answers, we studied the data. At the time, each new customer was being assigned a postsale consultant, who would set our service up and train the customer's staff in how to use it. Our first theory was that some of the postsale consultants were doing a better job than others. If we could identify which consultants were most successful, we could dig into their processes, understand what they were doing differently, and introduce the best practices across the team. However, when we examined customer churn by postsale consultant, the levels were similar across the team. That particular theory didn't check out.

Next we analyzed customer churn rates by salesperson. Eureka! Here was our answer. Across the organization, there was a more than 10-fold difference between the lowest and highest churn rates among salespeople. We did not have a customer onboarding problem. We had a sales problem. Our customer retention was predicated on the types of customers the salespeople chose to target and the expectations they set with each new account.

I immediately shared the analysis with the sales team, revealing each salesperson's churn rate and how it compared with the team average. I educated the team on the importance of retention, both to our business and to our customers. I said that I would be adjusting the sales compensation plan, in order to align customer retention performance with commission checks.

Sure enough, the next quarter I followed through on my promise. I stack-ranked the sales team from the person with the best retention rate right down to the person with the worst rate. Then I segmented the team into quartiles. The top-performing quartile would earn $4 per $1 of monthly recurring revenue from then on. "Congratulations," I said to this group. "I'm doubling your commission payments. Why? Because you bring in the best customers. Keep it up."

I moved on to the next quartile. "Good work," I said. "You now earn $3 per $1 of monthly recurring revenue—a 50% increase above your previous rate."

"For the folks in the third quartile, there is no change. You will be paid the same rate of $2 per $1 of monthly recurring revenue."

I concluded with the most difficult message. "For the fourth and worst-performing quartile, your earnings are cut to $1 per $1 of monthly recurring revenue. Why? Your customers are not succeeding. On average, they're unprofitable for our company. More important, you are wasting our customers' money by not setting proper expectations about how to succeed with our service. We have initiated training on better customer expectation setting. We need you to take that training seriously. We are here to help you through this skill development."

The combination of a different set of incentives and better training worked: Within six months, customer churn had dropped by 70%. Once again, a sales compensation plan had driven the results of the business.

3. The sustainable growth plan

Thanks in part to plan two, HubSpot had quickly closed in on product/market fit. Unrealistic expectations set by sales were now almost never among the reasons customers gave for quitting our service. Churn in general was far lower, and the reasons for cancellations were not alarming. It was time for our start-up to focus on achieving faster, profitable growth—in other words, scaling up the business. To do that, we had to align the sales compensation accordingly.

To ensure healthy growth, I needed to incorporate what we had already learned on our journey. I certainly wanted a strong incentive for the sales team to acquire new customers at a rapid clip. However, I needed to keep the team aligned with maximizing customer retention, since that would obviously offset acquisition costs and increase profitability.

One important insight we'd had earlier was that it was important for the customer to be committed to adopting inbound marketing. Though it can transform the way an organization gets its message to customers, inbound marketing is not a turnkey solution. It takes work. Customers must understand that to succeed. We had already worked to get salespeople to set realistic expectations, but we now

Boosting Performance with Sales Contests

CONTESTS ARE ALMOST AS EFFECTIVE as compensation plans when it comes to motivating the sales team. Contests bring a fun, dynamic aspect to a sometimes mundane daily routine. They can be designed to promote desired behaviors and, unlike commission plans, can be temporary. They can even be used to build team culture.

For these reasons, I ran a sales contest at HubSpot almost every month, especially in the early years of team development. Here are my six best practices for sales contest design:

1. **Align the contest with a short-term behavioral change.** For example, fearing a summer slump, you may want to boost activity in June. This increase would be difficult to pull off through the commission plan, but holding an activity-based contest for one month would do the trick.

2. **Make the contest team based.** This approach has a remarkable effect on team culture, especially early on. For the first three years at HubSpot, every contest I ran was a team contest. I'd often see high-performing salespeople help out teammates who were lagging, and the low performers would start working late to avoid letting their teams down. When I finally ran a contest based on individual performance, I heard accusations of cheating and saw backstabbing behavior for the first time. We immediately returned to team contests.

---

had to find a way to focus them on clients who would make a real investment (of time, energy, and money) in learning to use HubSpot's service. How could I align the sales team with this goal in a clear and measurable way?

The answer was advance-payment terms for new customers. When we looked at the data, we realized that our customers who paid month-to-month were less committed to the overall HubSpot service and were far more likely to defect. Those that prepaid annually were more committed to the service and ultimately were more successful. (Of course, advance payments also had a positive impact on HubSpot's cash flow—another factor that becomes important for a start-up as it reaches scale.)

As a result, our third plan was designed as follows: (1) Salespeople would earn $2 per $1 of monthly recurring revenue. (2) The

3. **Make the prize team based.** Choose a reward that the team experiences together: Rent a limo to take the winners to a casino. Buy them a golf outing. Send them sailing for a day. Making the prize team based maximizes the positive impact on culture. The winners return to the office with photos of the great time they had—together. People feel good about their colleagues. Teams feel motivated to win the following month.
4. **Send out updated contest standings daily.** At least once a day, publish the contest standings to the entire sales team (if not to the entire company), even if you have to compile and post them manually. This is such a critical execution point. Without daily updates, contest effectiveness will drop precipitously.
5. **Choose the time frame wisely.** The contest period needs to be long enough to bring about the desired behavioral change but short enough that salespeople stay engaged. A daily time frame is too short. Weeklong contests are on the briefer end of acceptable. A quarterly time frame is probably too long. Monthlong contests are ideal.
6. **Avoid contest fever.** Don't read this and implement five simultaneous contests. Overlapping contests will dilute one another. Run one contest at a time for a given group of salespeople.

commission would be paid out as follows: 50% on the customer's first month's payment, 25% on the sixth month's payment, and 25% on the 12th month's payment.

So if a customer signed up paying month-to-month, the salesperson would wait a full year to earn the last quarter of the commission for that customer. However, if the customer paid a full year's subscription in advance—a factor that was completely under the control of the salesperson—the entire commission would be earned immediately.

Before this plan was put in place, the average prepayment commitment was 2.5 months. After the plan was rolled out, that average jumped to seven months. Customer churn was checked; in fact, retention improved. The new customers were profitable to HubSpot. Salespeople felt in control of their destiny. Mission accomplished.

Before You Change the Comp Plan . . .

HubSpot is still a young and growing company, and we may have to adjust the sales compensation formula again as the business evolves. Drawing on what we've learned during our first eight years, my team has developed a few questions that we ask about any potential change: Is it simple? Is it aligned? And is it immediate?

Let me elaborate.

Simplicity

Salespeople should not need a spreadsheet to calculate their earnings. If too many variables are included, they may become confused about which behaviors will lead to the largest commission check. They might throw the plan aside and just go sell the way they know best. The opportunity to drive the desired behavior through the compensation plan is lost. Keep the plan simple. It should be extraordinarily clear which outcomes you are rewarding.

Alignment

Look ahead to the next year and ask yourself, "What is the most important goal the company needs to achieve? Customer count? Profitability? Customer success? Market share? New product distribution? New market penetration?" Once you've identified that goal, ask yourself, "How can the sales compensation plan be aligned with this objective?" Don't underestimate the power of the compensation plan. You can tweak sales training, redesign marketing materials, attend customer conferences—you name it. Regardless of those efforts, if the majority of your company's revenue is generated by salespeople, properly aligning their compensation plan will have greater impact than anything else will.

Immediacy

When salespeople succeed, they should see it reflected in their paychecks immediately. When they fail, they should feel the pain in their paychecks immediately. Any delay between good (or bad) behavior and the related financial outcome will decrease the impact of the plan.

Whenever I considered changing the compensation plan, I always involved the sales team in the redesign. To kick things off, I usually held a "town meeting" with the team. After communicating the goals for the plan, I would open up the floor to structural ideas. The brainstorming would begin. As the meeting progressed, I would share some of the structures that were being considered and invite people to offer their feedback.

As a follow-up, I often created a page on the company wiki, reiterating the reasons for changing the plan, stating the goals, and describing some of the structures that were being considered. The conversation would then continue online with ideas and reactions. I responded to most comments. This digital format allowed salespeople to catch up on and participate in the conversation when they had time.

Throughout the process, I was very explicit that the commission plan design was not a democratic process. It was critical that the salespeople did not confuse transparency and involvement with an invitation to selfishly design the plan around their own needs. Most of them appreciated the openness, even when changes were not favorable to their individual situations. During the process the sales team contributed some great ideas. Each commission plan change we made included at least one structural element that had originated from a salesperson during our discussions. Because of this involvement, when a new plan was rolled out, the sales team would understand why the final structure had been chosen.

Compensation is just one of the tools I learned to use while scaling up HubSpot's sales force. Our hiring, training, and sales coaching programs have also been vital to our success. The common thread among them is that they rely on close analysis of what works and what doesn't, rigorous use of data and metrics instead of intuition or improvisation, and systematically reducing what does work into a formula that can be replicated.

Am I recommending the same evolution of compensation plans for every business? Absolutely not. The sales compensation plan should reflect the type of business you're in and the stage of business you're at. The evolution of HubSpot's plan illustrates this point and provides a real-world example of the impact that a change in plan can have on business results. It also illustrates how, in an era when managers can access data on everything that happens inside their firms, successfully managing a sales force should be much less of an art and much more of a science.

Originally published in April 2015. Reprint R1504E

How to *Really* Motivate Salespeople

by Doug J. Chung

BEFORE I BECAME A BUSINESS school professor, I worked as a management consultant. One engagement in particular had a profound influence on my career. The project involved working with the Asia-based sales force of a global consumer products company. This company practiced "route sales," which meant reps spent their days visiting mom-and-pop convenience stores, servicing accounts. One thing about the organization surprised me: Its sales managers spent inordinate time listening to the reps complain about their compensation.

The complaints were based on what the reps saw as a myriad of problems. Their quotas were set too high, so they couldn't possibly reach them. Or their territory was subpar, limiting their ability to sign new accounts. Sometimes the complaints focused on fairness: A rep who was hitting his quotas and making decent money would want a manager to do something about a "lazy" colleague who was earning outsize pay simply because he had a good territory. Imagine any conceivable complaint a salesperson might have about pay, and I guarantee that sales managers at my client's company had heard it.

The reps weren't the only ones obsessed with the compensation system. The company liked to play around with the system's components to try to find better ways to motivate reps and boost revenue, or to increase the return on the money it spent paying salespeople—a large part of its marketing budget. This company's sales comp system was fairly basic: Reps earned a salary and a commission of around 1% of sales. The company worried that the system was too focused on outcomes and might over- or under-reward reps for factors outside their control. So it began basing compensation on their effort and behavior, not just on top-line sales. For instance, under the new system, a portion of compensation was based on customer satisfaction surveys, the number of prospective accounts visited (even if they didn't buy), and the retention of existing accounts.

Largely because of this consulting assignment, I became so curious about the best ways to compensate salespeople that I began reading academic articles on the subject. Eventually I pursued a PhD in marketing at Yale, where I studied the theory and practice of how companies can and should manage and pay salespeople—research I now continue at Harvard Business School.

Although there are fewer academics studying sales force compensation and management than researching trendy marketing subjects, such as the use of social media or digital advertising, in the past decade it's become a fast-moving field. While some of the basic theories established in the 1970s and 1980s still apply, academics have begun testing those theories using two methods new to this area of research: empirical analysis of companies' sales and pay data, and field experiments in which researchers apply various pay structures to different groups of salespeople and then compare the groups' effort and output.

This new wave of research is already providing evidence that some standard compensation practices probably hurt sales. For instance, the research suggests that caps on commissions, which most large companies use, decrease high-performing reps' motivation and effort. Likewise, the practice of "ratcheting" quotas (raising a salesperson's annual quota if he or she exceeded it the previous year) may hurt long-term results. Research based on field experiments (as opposed to the lab experiments academics have been doing for many years) is also yielding new insight into how the timing and labeling of bonuses can affect salespeople's motivation.

In this article I will take readers through the evolution of this research and suggest the best ways to apply it. With luck, this

Idea in Brief

The Research

In the past decade, researchers studying sales force compensation have been moving out of the lab into the field, doing empirical analysis of companies' pay and sales data and conducting experiments with actual reps.

The Findings

Companies sell more when they remove caps on commissions; "ratcheting"—raising a rep's quota after a good year—dampens motivation; and a pay system with multiple components (such as various kinds of bonuses and commissions) can engage a broad range of salespeople.

The Implications

Many companies use experiments to improve pricing, marketing, and website design. Because sales compensation is a large expense and sales force effectiveness is a primary revenue driver, companies should apply analytics and experimentation to find better ways to pay and motivate their salespeople, too.

---

knowledge not only will help companies think about better ways to compensate salespeople, but also might mean that their managers spend fewer hours listening to them gripe about unfair pay.

The Dangers of Complex Compensation Systems

Researchers studying sales force compensation have long been guided by the principal-agent theory. This theory, drawn from the field of economics, describes the problem that results from conflicting interests between a principal (a company, for instance) and an agent hired by that principal (an employee). For example, a company wants an employee's maximum output, but a salaried employee may be tempted to slack off and may be able to get away with it if the company can't observe how hard the employee is working. Most incentive or variable pay schemes—including stock options for the C-suite—are attempts to align the interests of principals and agents. Commission-based plans for salespeople are just one example.

Salespeople were paid by commission for centuries before economists began writing about the principal-agent problem. Companies chose this system for at least three reasons. First, it's easy to measure the short-term output of a salesperson, unlike that of most workers. Second, field reps have traditionally worked with little (if any) supervision; commission-based pay gives managers some control, making up for their inability to know if a rep is actually visiting clients or playing golf. Third, studies of personality type show that salespeople typically have a larger appetite for risk than other workers, so a pay plan that offers upside potential appeals to them.

During the 1980s several important pieces of research influenced firms' use of commission-based systems. One, by my Harvard colleague Rajiv Lal and several coauthors, explored how the level of uncertainty in an industry's sales cycle should influence pay systems. They found that the more uncertain a firm's sales cycle, the more a salesperson's pay should be based on a fixed salary; the less uncertain the cycle, the more pay should depend on commission. Consider Boeing, whose salespeople can spend years talking with an airline before it actually places an order for new 787s. A firm like that would struggle to retain reps if pay depended mostly on commissions. In contrast, industries in which sales happen quickly and frequently (a door-to-door salesperson may have a chance to book revenue every hour) and in which sales correlate more directly with effort and so are less characterized by uncertainty, pay mostly (if not entirely) on commission. This research still drives how companies think about the mix between salaries and commissions.

Another important study, from the late 1980s, came from the economists Bengt Holmstrom and Paul Milgrom. In their very theoretical paper, which relies on a lot of assumptions, they found that a formula of straight-line commissions (in which salespeople earn commissions at the same rate no matter how much they sell) is generally the optimal way to pay reps. They argue that if you make a sales comp formula too complicated—with lots of bonuses or changes in commission structure triggered by hitting goals within a certain period—reps will find ways to game it. The most common method of doing that is to play with the timing of sales. If a salesperson needs to make a yearly quota, for instance, she might ask a friendly client to allow her to book a sale that would ordinarily be made in January during the final days of December instead (this is known as "pulling"); a rep who's already hit quota, in contrast, might be tempted to "push" December sales into January to get a head start on the next year's goal.

While a very simple comp plan such as the one advocated by Holmstrom and Milgrom can be appealing (for one thing, it's easier and less costly to administer), many companies opt for something more complex. They do so in recognition that each salesperson is unique, with individual motivations and needs, so a system with multiple components may be more attractive to a broad group of reps. In fact, to get the optimal work out of a particular salesperson, you should in theory design a compensation system tailored to that individual. For instance, some people are more motivated by cash, others by recognition, and still others by a noncash reward like a ski trip or a gift card. Some respond better to quarterly bonuses, while others are more productive if they focus on an annual quota. However, such an individualized plan would be extremely difficult and costly to administer, and companies fear the "watercooler effect": Reps might share information about their compensation with one another, which could raise concerns about fairness and lead to resentment. So for now, individualized plans remain uncommon.

Concerns about fairness create other pressures when designing comp plans. For instance, companies realize that success in any field, including sales, involves a certain amount of luck. If a rep for a soft-drink company has a territory in which a Walmart is opening, her sales (and commission) will increase, but she's not responsible for the revenue jump—so in essence the company is paying her for being lucky. But when a salesperson's compensation decreases owing to bad luck, he or she may get upset and leave the firm. That attrition can be a problem. So even though there are downsides to making a compensation system more complex, many companies have done so in the hope of appealing to different types of salespeople and limiting the impact of luck by utilizing caps or compensating people for inputs or effort (such as number of calls made) instead of simply for closing sales.

How to create a sales comp plan

Sales compensation plans need to support a company's strategy; motivate a broad range of performers; be fair and simple to explain and understand; and result in payouts that are within a company's budget. Here are the steps sales managers must take to design a plan that meets those criteria.

Step 1: Set the pay level	Step 2: Balance salary and incentives	Step 3: Design the plan			Step 4: Choose payout periods	Step 5: Consider additional elements
		Metrics	**Plan type**	**Payout curve**		
This is crucial for attracting and retaining talent.	The proportion of earnings that comes from salary and from incentives determines the riskiness of the plan. The proper balance varies by industry and is often based on the degree of certainty that a salesperson's efforts will directly influence sales.	Most companies still pay salespeople a commission based on gross revenue, although some companies pay on the basis of profitability of sales.	Many companies supplement salary and commissions with bonuses based on exceeding quotas or reaching other goals.	Caps on earnings limit the pay of top performers and flatten the payout curve (or make it "regressive"); accelerators or overachievement commissions ramp up the pay of top performers, creating a "progressive" structure.	Companies can set quotas and bonus structures to cover periods ranging from a single week to an entire year. Research shows that shorter payout periods help keep low performers motivated and engaged.	Many companies use nonmonetary incentives, such as contests or recognition programs.

Source: Adapted from The Power of Sales Analytics, *by Andris A. Zoltners, Prabhakant Sinha, and Sally E. Lorimer*

Using Real Company Data to Build Understanding

The big difference between earlier research on sales compensation and the research that's come out in the past decade is that the latter is not based just on theories. Although companies tend to be very secretive about their pay plans, researchers have begun persuading them to share data. And companies have been opening up to academics, partly because of the attention being given to big data; managers hope that allowing researchers to apply high-powered math and estimation techniques to their numbers will help them develop better tools to motivate their workforce. Indeed, these new empirical studies have revealed some surprises, but they have also confirmed some of what we already believed about the best ways to pay.

Tom Steenburgh, a professor at the University of Virginia's Darden School of Business, published one of the first of these papers, in 2008. He persuaded a B2B firm selling office equipment to give him several years of sales and compensation information. This unique data set allowed Steenburgh to look at sales and pay data for individual salespeople and use it to make assumptions about how pay influences behavior. The company had a complex compensation plan: Reps earned a salary, commissions, quarterly bonuses based on hitting quotas, an additional yearly bonus, and an "overachievement" commission that kicked in once they passed certain sales goals. He focused on the issue of timing games: Was there evidence that salespeople were pushing or pulling sales from one quarter to another to help them hit their quotas and earn incentive pay? That's a really important question, because pushing and pulling don't increase a firm's revenue, and so paying salespeople extra for doing that is a waste.

Even though the salespeople in the study could receive (or miss out on) substantial bonuses for hitting (or missing) quotas, Steenburgh found no evidence of timing games. He concluded that the firm's customers required sales to close according to their own needs (at the end of a quarter or a year, say) and that the firm's managers were able to keep close enough tabs on the reps to prevent them from influencing the timing of sales in a way that would boost their incentive payments. That finding was significant, because quotas and bonuses are a large part of most sales compensation plans.

In 2011 Sanjog Misra, of UCLA, and Harikesh Nair, of Stanford, published a study that analyzed the sales comp plan of a *Fortune* 500 optical products company. In contrast with the firm Steenburgh studied, this company had a relatively simple plan: It paid a salary plus a standard commission on sales after achieving quota, and it capped how much a rep could earn in order to prevent windfalls from really big sales. Such caps are relatively common in large companies.

As they analyzed the data, Misra and Nair concluded that the cap was hurting overall sales and that the company would be better off removing it. They also determined that many reps' motivation was hurt by the firm's practice of ratcheting. Setting and adjusting quotas is a very sensitive piece of the sales compensation formula, and there's disagreement over ratcheting: Some feel that if you don't adjust quotas, you're making it too easy for reps to earn big commissions and bonuses, while others argue that if you raise a person's quota after a very strong year, you're effectively penalizing your top performers.

Misra and Nair estimated that if this firm removed the cap on sales reps' earnings and eliminated quotas, sales would increase by 8%. The company implemented those recommendations, and the next year companywide revenue rose by 9%.

A third empirical study of sales rep pay, on which I am the lead author, was published in *Marketing Science* in 2014. Like Steenburgh, we utilized data from a B2B office equipment supplier with a complex compensation plan. We examined how the components of the plan affected various kinds of reps: high performers, low performers, and middle-of-the-road performers.

We found that although the salary and straight commission affected the three groups in similar ways, the other components created different incentives that appealed to certain subsets of the sales force. For instance, overachievement commissions were important for keeping the highest performers motivated and engaged after they'd hit their quotas. Quarterly bonuses were most important for the lower performers: Whereas the high performers could be effectively incentivized by a yearly quota and bonus, more-frequent goals helped keep lower performers on track. Some people compare the way people compensate a sales force to the way teachers motivate students: Top students will do fine in a course in which the entire grade is determined by a final exam, but lower-performing students need frequent quizzes and tests during the semester to motivate them to keep up. Our study showed that the same general rule applies to sales compensation.

Our research also suggested that the firm would benefit if it shifted from quarterly bonuses to *cumulative* quarterly bonuses. For example, say a salesperson is supposed to sell 300 units in the first quarter and 300 units in the second quarter. Under a regular quarterly plan, a salesperson who misses that number in the first quarter but sells 300 units in the second quarter will still get the second-quarter bonus. Under a cumulative system, the rep needs to have cumulative (year-to-date) sales of 600 units to get the second-quarter bonus, regardless of his first-quarter performance. Cumulative quotas do a better job of keeping reps motivated during periods in which they're showing poor results, because reps know that even if they're going to miss their number, any sales they can squeeze out will help them reach their cumulative number for the next period. In fact, even before we made our recommendations to the company in our study, managers there decided to move to cumulative quotas.

Out of the Lab, into the Field

In addition to sharing sales and compensation data with academics, companies in the past several years have been allowing controlled, short-term field experiments in which researchers adjust reps' pay and measure the effects. Prior to the use of field experiments, most academic experiments regarding sales force compensation took place in labs and involved volunteers (usually undergraduates) rather than real salespeople. Shifting from this artificial setting into actual companies helps make the results of these studies more practical and convincing.

As an example of one such experiment, consider recent work my colleague Das Narayandas and I did with a South Asian company that has a retail sales force for its consumer durable products. The company uses a simple system of linear commissions—reps earn a fixed percentage of sales, with no quotas, bonuses, or overachievement commissions. Managers were interested in seeing how instituting bonuses would affect the reps' performance, so over six months we tested various ways to frame and time bonuses—always comparing results against a control group.

For one of our experimental groups, we created a bonus that was payable at the end of the week if a rep sold six units. For another group, we framed the bonus differently, using the well-known concept of loss aversion, which posits that the pain people feel from a loss exceeds the happiness they feel from a gain. Instead of telling reps they would receive a bonus *if* they sold six units, we told them they would receive a bonus *unless* they failed to sell at least six units. To test the concept even further, the company's managers suggested another experiment in which we paid the bonuses at the beginning of the week and then had the reps return the money if they missed the goal.

The results showed that all three types of bonuses exerted similar effects and that in every case the group receiving the bonus generally outsold the control group. Loss aversion didn't have much effect. We believe that's partly because we were using cash, which is liquid and interchangeable; in the future we might experiment with noncash rewards, such as physical objects.

We also tried to measure the impact on sales reps' effort of cash payments that were framed as gifts (as opposed to bonuses). Whereas bonuses are viewed as transactional, research shows that framing something as a gift creates a particular form of goodwill between the giver and recipient. In our study we used cash but told employees it was a gift because there were no strings attached—they didn't have to meet a quota to receive it. We found that the timing of a gift directly influences how reps respond: If you give the gift at the beginning of a period, they view it as a reward for past performance and tend to slack off. If you tell them they will receive a gift at the end of a period, they work harder. We concluded that if companies want to encourage that kind of reciprocity, they need to pay careful attention to timing.

Other researchers are using field experiments to better understand how salespeople react to changes in payment schemes, but most of this work is so new that it hasn't been published yet. One paper presented at a conference in 2014 showed that if salespeople receive cash incentives for passing tests about the product they are selling, they will sell more. (This is an example of sales compensation based on effort as opposed to results.) Another recent field experiment found that sales reps valued noncash incentives (such as points that could be used for vacations or for items such as televisions) more than the actual monetary cost of the good the points could purchase. As more researchers and companies embrace the use of field experiments, sales managers will learn even more about the best ways to motivate their teams.

It Pays to Experiment

After spending a decade in academia studying sales force compensation, I sometimes wonder what would happen if I were transported back into my job as a management consultant. What would I tell sales force managers to do differently?

Some of my advice would be straightforward: I would urge managers to remove the caps on commissions or, if they have to retain some ceiling for political reasons, to set it as high as possible. The research is clear on this point: Companies sell more when they eliminate thresholds at which salespeople's marginal incentives are reduced. There might be problems if some reps' earnings dramatically exceed their bosses' or even rival a C-suite executive's compensation, but the evidence shows that firms benefit when these arbitrary caps are removed.

I would tell sales managers to be extremely careful in setting and adjusting quotas. For instance, the research clearly shows that ratcheting quotas is detrimental. It's tempting to look at a sales rep who blows through her yearly number and conclude that the quota must be too low—and quotas do need to be adjusted from time to time. But in general it's important to prevent reps from feeling that unfairness or luck plays a part in compensation, and resetting quotas can contribute to that perception. And if something outside the salesperson's control—such as an economic downturn—made it more difficult to hit a goal, I would consider reducing the quota in the middle of the year. It's important to keep quotas at the right level to properly motivate people.

On the basis of my own research, I would advocate for a pay system with multiple components—one that's not overly complicated but has enough elements (such as quarterly performance bonuses and overachievement bonuses) to keep high performers, low performers, and average performers motivated and engaged throughout the year.

Finally, I would urge my client companies to consider experimenting with their pay systems. Over the past decade managers have become attuned to the value of experimentation (A/B testing, in particular); today many consumer goods companies experiment constantly to try to optimize pricing. There are important lessons to be learned from doing controlled experiments on sales reps' pay, because the behaviors encouraged by changes in incentives can exert a large influence on a firm's revenue, and because sales force compensation is a large cost that should be managed as efficiently as possible. Involving academic researchers in these experiments can be beneficial: Having a trained researcher take the lead generally will result in a more controlled environment, a more scientific process, and more-robust findings. These studies also help the world at large, because research that improves how companies motivate salespeople will result in better and more-profitable businesses for employees and shareholders.

Originally published in April 2015. Reprint R1504C

Getting Beyond "Show Me the Money"

An interview with Andris Zoltners by Daniel McGinn

AS A YOUNG BUSINESS SCHOOL PROFESSOR, Andris Zoltners became fascinated by two questions: How many salespeople does a company need, and how should it divide up their territories to balance workload and market potential—so as to maximize profits? To unearth the answers, he developed and applied complex math models, and in 1983 Zoltners, by then a professor at Northwestern University's Kellogg School, had enough companies clamoring for his insights that he and a colleague, Prabha Sinha, founded ZS Associates. Today the firm is one of the world's largest sales consultancies, with 3,500 employees, and Zoltners, now emeritus after 35 years on Northwestern's faculty, is considered an authority on the best ways to manage and pay a sales force. He has coauthored six books on the subject; the latest, *The Power of Sales Analytics,* was published last summer. Zoltners recently spoke to HBR's Daniel McGinn about why companies rely too heavily on compensation systems to drive results, why field managers are the key to a high-performing sales force, and what's changed over the years he's spent watching the field. Here are some edited highlights of that conversation:

HBR: *What are the most common mistakes companies make in compensating a sales force?*

Zoltners: Too often they over- or underincentivize key products, resulting in misdirected sales force efforts—that's a classic mistake.

Or they underpay their top performers: You have to "feed the eagles." Sometimes they overpay salespeople with good territories—they pay for the territory and not the talent. Or companies set goals or quotas too low or too high. If they're too low, people blow right through them and earn a big payday without having to work particularly hard, and once they're accustomed to that level of pay it's very difficult to wean them off it. On the other hand, if the quotas are too high, people will give up and stop working. They'll put off sales to the next pay period, when the goal is lower. Companies have gotten better at quota setting over the past 30 years, partly because better data for measuring territory potential is available. And they've improved at designing incentive plans because they can use analytics, and more expertise is available. With analytics you can start to estimate the consequences of what will happen if you change a plan, rather than guessing. You can look not only at overall revenue but also at who gets helped and who gets hurt by changes. If your best performers will be hurt by a new plan, you want to know that before you implement it.

Do sales leaders rely too much on compensation as a motivator?

To give you some context, 85% of companies will change their sales compensation plan this year. They're not just changing the quotas—these are structural changes. So why do they do it? Some of them are entering new markets or introducing new products, and they need to focus the sales team on new opportunities. Strategic opportunities must be addressed. But the reality is that while there are various drivers of sales success—you can restructure the sales force, hire better reps, select different sales managers, offer more-effective coaching—many of them take a long time to have an effect. Though it's only one driver, changing a compensation plan is relatively easy, and it can get quick results. It's also an area where there's always room for improvement—it's hard to get right. When you create a plan, it's almost impossible not to overpay some people and underpay others. And rest assured, the latter group will find out about it and argue for changes.

Should different reps have different pay plans?

I have colleagues who argue that someday we'll see customized individual comp plans, where salespeople will be able to choose the features and rewards they want. I'm not sure if I agree. The risk is that some salespeople will make the wrong choices and feel regret. The company also may pay out more than it needs to.

Do most companies have the right degree of "leverage," or at-risk pay, in their incentive plans?

Some companies don't really understand how leveraged their plans are, because of "free sales"—sales that occur this year but are due to past effort in the territory. In many product categories, if you sell something one year, there's a high probability you'll make residual sales the next year without any effort. If a salesperson is paid a commission or bonus for free sales, we call that a "hidden salary," since it's an incentive paid for something that's nearly automatic. Many companies don't account for hidden salaries when they design their comp plans and set goals. A company may think that it's paying salespeople 60% in salary and 40% in commissions, so people have strong incentives to sell. But if the salespeople have a lot of free sales, they may really be earning 85% in salary and 15% in commissions, which is a lower incentive.

You've argued that many sales compensation plans are too complicated. Why do companies favor complexity?

That is a significant problem with many plans. I've seen plans that have different payments for as many as 28 different objectives. This happens because multiple market managers need to gain sales force attention for their brands. But people can't focus on that many things—four or five goals are the maximum, and any feature that affects less than 15% of someone's incentive pay is probably going to be ignored because it's not meaningful. Some people argue that companies with a complex sales process or lots of product offerings need a complex pay plan, but I don't believe that's true. IBM has a complex selling process and sells many complicated products and services. But its pay plan has three components, and you can describe it on one side of a business card. That's the way a good plan should work.

Has the quality or attitude of the people going into sales changed during your years in the field?

A sales force usually spans different generations with different job expectations. Millennials may want a higher quality of life and more meaning in their work. They expect to communicate electronically and constantly and crave frequent feedback on how they're doing. Baby Boomers want to ensure a comfortable retirement. Those in the middle may be working for financial security. A successful compensation plan needs to accommodate all those objectives.

Should companies base pay on activities, like number of calls made, instead of on sales?

No. In most industries salespeople earn a good salary before the incentives kick in. That salary is paying for activity—for making the sales calls. Paying salespeople for performing the basic duties of the job is an abdication of management; the manager is supposed to ensure that those activities are done. There are at least two more reasons not to pay for activity. First, it's difficult to measure: People report it when it's convenient and may mistake what they actually do. Second, tracking activity will motivate an increase in quantity but also trigger a decrease in quality.

How big a problem is disintermediation, or the diminished role of salespeople in actually generating revenue?

It's a problem. We describe it using two concepts. The first is causality: If you can't affect the outcome, you shouldn't be rewarded for outcomes. Does an auto salesperson really cause you to buy a car, or is he just negotiating the discount and doing the paperwork, since you probably decided what to buy by reading websites before you walked into the showroom? The other is measurability—can you accurately measure the sales and profit generated by a single salesperson? Particularly in B2B sales, where large sales teams service national accounts, it's hard to measure the contribution of an individual. I have met salespeople who say they have no idea how their commission checks are calculated, because they're part of a team and credit is divided up by an obtuse algorithm somewhere. For incentives to really work, you need to have individual causality and measurability, and in a lot of industries those are declining. There's some argument that, as a result, companies need to cut back on incentive pay. So far most companies haven't done that, because the incentives are built into the culture and firms are afraid that if they remove them, they'll lose their best salespeople.

Is globalization changing the way companies pay their salespeople?

Some global companies want to use the same sales compensation plan around the world. I can't imagine how that would work. You're going to pay people in the United States, Thailand, Mexico, and Denmark the same way? The tax systems are completely different—in Scandinavia, incentive payments are taxed much higher than salary is, so people there would be penalized by a high-incentive plan. China, India, and Latin America prefer higher-risk plans. That being said, it's useful to have some global incentive-compensation guidelines and frameworks to help local teams make good choices about how they pay their salespeople—choices that reflect the needs and culture of their specific market but also are aligned with overall company business and compensation strategies and philosophies.

Over the past decade there's been a lot of discussion of changing sales methodologies—for instance, the shift from "solution selling" to "challenger selling." Is that important?

It's all the same stuff—it just gets packaged in a different way. I worry that some sales methods are too prescriptive—they want to come up with an approach you can use with every customer. Some sales leaders like a prescribed approach because it allows them to control activity, but salespeople aren't robots. My view is that customers are different, and salespeople need to understand each customer's needs and be adaptive. It might be better if the industry would focus more on what really drives sales success—broader issues like hiring and managing—instead of focusing on exactly what salespeople should say to close a deal.

Why are field sales managers so important?

Many firms move their best salespeople into sales management jobs, but the skills don't necessarily translate. Managing someone is never easy. If I tell you that you're doing a terrible job with this interview, do you really want to hear it? Some people are responsive to criticism; others are defensive. Managers also have to work through a salesperson—they can't make the sale themselves—and that can be challenging. In sales it's about me, what I do. In management it's about you and how I can help you succeed. Good managers empower their people to do the selling. Also, sales managers who are promoted from within are usually friends with the people they're managing, which makes it harder. But the role is incredibly important. If you have a bad salesperson, it affects one territory. If you have a bad sales manager, it affects a whole district.

A lot of your consulting work involves using math to optimize how companies sell, but it's striking how much you talk about soft issues—especially culture—as a driver of results.

That's true—culture is really important. The best sales leaders shape culture by modeling behavior and telling stories. I once had the vice president of sales for a defibrillator company speak to my class at Northwestern. He showed up looking really tired. It turned out he'd spent all night riding around Chicago in an ambulance, because he wanted to see how customers used his products. That illustrated his commitment to listening to customers. Stories like that get around. Cultures are really about choices—the culture pushes you to do this or do that. The compensation plan is a piece of the culture—it's telling people what choices the company wants them to make. That being said, I think that sales analytics is important, and it's getting more important in the age of big data.

How well do tech start-ups manage their sales forces?
Many of them need help. A lot of them hire leaders who are very smart people but who have very little selling experience. They focus on doing everything very fast, and if it doesn't work, you just fix it later. Leading a sales force requires understanding the sales system, and in new industries and new companies, there's often too little of that. Fixing it later is very difficult to do well.

Some innovation experts point to salespeople as an important source of ideas. Do many companies really use them in that way?
Salespeople won't play that role unless you have systems in place to capture that information. Generating ideas isn't natural or inherent to what they do. But they do gather information, and companies should build procedures to find out what they're hearing from customers.

Is the number of salespeople going to decline because of technology and self-service?
People have predicted that before, and they were wrong. We're hearing those predictions again. The sales job will certainly change. Social media, e-mail, videoconferencing, and webinars are all ways that companies are connecting with customers and prospects. There will be more telesales and inside sales jobs, and more national account or key account jobs. In many industries there may be less face-to-face selling. But on the seller's side, there needs to be a captain, someone in charge of that interaction. That will remain the role of the salesperson. In business, nothing happens until a sale is made, and most jobs involve some form of selling. As a professor, I'm selling ideas. Selling is about being curious and trying to help people. It's a role that shows up in unexpected places. I had a knee replacement, and there was a sales guy in the operating room, making sure the doctor used the right components. That's a pretty critical job, isn't it?

Final thoughts?

You know, it's not all about incentives. You manage through culture. You manage through managers. You manage by sizing, structuring, territory design, training, and hiring—there are many decisions that drive sales force effectiveness. There's this idea that unless you put a quarter in, you're not going to get anything out of someone—that people are coin operated. We have to build a new paradigm.

Originally published in April 2015. Reprint R1504F

About the Contributors

BRENT ADAMSON is a managing director at Corporate Executive Board.

JAMES C. ANDERSON is the William L. Ford Professor of Marketing and Wholesale Distribution at Northwestern University's Kellogg School of Management.

ANNA BIRD is a director of strategic research for CEB Marketing.

THOMAS V. BONOMA was a professor of marketing at Harvard Business School, in Boston, and the founder of Renaissance Cosmetics, in Stamford, Connecticut. He authored several books and HBR articles.

DOUG J. CHUNG is an assistant professor of marketing at Harvard Business School.

MATTHEW DIXON is an executive director at Corporate Executive Board.

MANISH GOYAL is a partner at McKinsey in Dallas.

MARYANNE Q. HANCOCK is a partner at McKinsey in Atlanta.

HOMAYOUN HATAMI is a partner at McKinsey in Paris and a coauthor of *Sales Growth: Five Proven Strategies from the World's Sales Leaders* (Wiley, 2012).

PHILIP KOTLER is the S.C. Johnson & Son Distinguished Professor of International Marketing at Northwestern University's Kellogg School of Management in Evanston, Illinois.

SUJ KRISHNASWAMY is the founder and a principal of Stinsights (www.stinsights.com), a Chicago-based business strategy and market research firm specializing in sales-marketing interface.

ABOUT THE CONTRIBUTORS

SALLY E. LORIMER is a marketing and sales consultant and a business writer based in Northville, Michigan. Lorimer, Zoltners, and Sinha are the authors of three books on sales force management.

JAMES A. NARUS is a professor of business marketing at Wake Forest University.

NEIL RACKHAM is a visiting professor at the University of Portsmouth in England, the author of *Spin Selling* (McGraw-Hill, 1988), and a coauthor of *Rethinking the Sales Force* (McGraw-Hill, 1999).

MARK ROBERGE is the chief revenue officer of HubSpot, a Boston-based inbound marketing firm. "The Right Way to Use Compensation" is adapted from his book, *The Sales Acceleration Formula* (2015), with permission of its publisher, Wiley.

KARL SCHMIDT is the practice manager of CEB Marketing.

PRABHAKANT SINHA is a cochairman of ZS Associates. Sinha, Zoltners, and Lorimer are the authors of three books on sales force management.

NICHOLAS TOMAN is a research director at Corporate Executive Board.

MARC WOUTERS is a professor of management accounting at Karlsruhe Institute of Technology, in Germany, and at the University of Amsterdam, in the Netherlands.

ANDRIS A. ZOLTNERS is a professor of marketing at Northwestern University's Kellogg School of Management in Evanston, Illinois. He is also a cochairman of ZS Associates, a global business-consulting firm headquartered in Evanston. Zoltners, Sinha, and Lorimer are the authors of three books on sales force management.

Index

account managers, 61-62
Adamson, Brent, 67-82, 101-114, 127-138
advertising, costs of, 27-28
advocates, 74-76, 131-132
alignment, between sales and marketing, 33-37
Anderson, James C., 115-125
at-risk pay, 163
attraction power, 10, 11, 12
authority, 11, 13
Automatic Data Processing (ADP), 81

Baby Boomers, 164
benefits, 14-16
big data, 84-85, 92, 95-99, 155
Bird, Anna, 127-138
"Blockers," 77, 79
Bonoma, Thomas V., 1-21
bonuses, 153, 155-158
brand awareness, 40, 41
brand consideration, 40
brand preference, 40, 41
break-even ratio, for sales force size, 56
business creation, 123-124
business growth, 143-145
business jets, 3-5
business life cycle, sales force structure and, 45-65
business value, 132
buyers
　behavioral clues for identifying, 13-14
　gathering psychological intelligence on, 18-21
　motivations of, 14-16
　perceptions of, 16-18
　powerful, 9-14
　self-interest of, 3, 14
　See also customers
buying center, 5-9, 13-14

buying funnel, 40
buying process
　achieving consensus in, 127-138
　changes in, 101
　human factors in, 2-5
　key players in, 4, 5-14
　multiple decision makers in, 104, 127-138
　psychology of, 1-21

carryover sales percentage, 57-58
"Challengers," 72-73
challenger selling, 165-166
change, culture of, 55
chief customer officer (CCO), 39
chief revenue officer (CRO), 39
Chung, Doug J., 149-160
"Climbers," 77, 80
coaching, 111
coercive power, 10-11
collaboration, 95, 96-98, 105
commission-based pay, 151-153.
　See also compensation
commission caps, 150, 151, 156, 159
common ground, identifying, among stakeholders, 132-134
communication
　informal, 111
　between sales and marketing, 35-36
compensation
　at-risk pay, 163
　based on activities, 164
　bonuses, 153, 155-158
　commission caps, 150, 151, 156, 159
　customized pay plans, 163
　globalization and, 165
　vs. intrinsic rewards, 113-114
　mistakes in, 161-162
　as motivator, 149-160, 162
　organizational culture and, 166-167

INDEX

compensation (*continued*)
   overly complex plans, 151–153, 163–164
   plans for, 154
   salaries, 152, 164
   strategies for using, 139–148
   using data on, 155–160
competitive advantage, 28, 29, 120–121
compliance sales climate, 109, 110
consensus sales, 127–138
corporate culture, 12, 111, 166–167
corporate jet purchases, 3–5
critical thinking skills, 112
cross-functional collaboration, 96–98
culture
   of change, 55
   organizational, 12, 111, 166–167
cumulative quotas, 157
customer acquisition plan, 140–141
customer agility, 71
customer retention, 141–143
customers
   achieving consensus in, 127–138
   business priorities of, 122–123
   coaching on how to buy, 80–82
   connecting with emotions of, 136–137
   emerging needs of, 71
   identifying justifiers for, 119–123
   informed, 102, 115
   misunderstanding, by suppliers, 116–118
   redefining needs of, 71–73
   selling to empowered, 104
   stakeholders, 74–80, 105, 127–138
   upending traditional ways of thinking in, 72–73
   See also buyers
customer-verified sales funnel, 107–108

data analysis, 84–85, 93–99, 155–157, 162
data management, 95
deciders, 7, 8
decision makers
   consensus among multiple, 104, 127–138
   determining, 3
   insight selling and, 102
defined relationship, between sales and marketing, 29, 33, 34, 35
disintermediation, 164–165
distinctive features, 116–117
Dixon, Matthew, 67–82, 101–114

emotional intelligence, 112
employee productivity, 110–111
empowered customers, 104
established demand, 70–74
expert power, 10, 11

fairness, in compensation plans, 153
features, 116–117
feedback, from sales force, 37
field experiments, on compensation, 157–159
free sales, 163
"Friends," 77, 79

gatekeepers, 6, 7
gifts, 158–159
globalization, 165
"Go-Getters," 76, 77–78, 79
Goyal, Manish, 83–99
growth phase, sales force in, 52–58
growth pockets, 84–90
"Guides," 77, 79

172

INDEX

Hancock, Maryanne Q., 83–99
Homayoun, Hatami, 83–99
hot buttons, 15–16
HubSpot, compensation plan of, 139–147
human factors, in buying decisions, 2–5

IBM, 24
inbound marketing, 143–144
influencers, 6, 7, 8
informal communication, 111
initiators, 6, 7
innovation, 106, 167
insight selling, 70, 72–73, 102–104, 112–114
integration, between sales and marketing, 33, 37–43

job rotation, 36
joint assignments, 36
judgment-oriented sales climate, 105–114
justifiers, 115–123
   defined, 115–116
   discovering, 119–123
   identifying fresh, 124–125
   new business creation and, 123–124

knowledge workers, 105
Kotler, Philip, 23–44
Krishnaswamy, Suj, 23–44

language mapping, 133
liaison, between sales and marketing, 36
long-term focus, 112

Lorimer, Sally E., 45–65
loss aversion, 158

managerial coaching, 111
marketing
   budget, 27–28
   four P's of, 26, 27
   funnel, 39, 41
   inbound, 143–144
   metrics, 42–43
   in micromarkets, 96
   relationship between sales and, 23–44, 96–98, 138
   roles for, 25–27
   splitting, into upstream/downstream, 41–42
   support for mobilizers by, 137–138
market share
   causes of differences in, 89
   gauging, 88
market teams, 108–109
mature companies, sales force in, 59–62
McGinn, Daniel, 161–168
micromarkets, 83–100
   aligning sales coverage with opportunity, 91–92
   data analysis for, 95–99
   defining size of, 86
   determining growth potential of, 87
   gauging market share of, 88
   growth pockets, 84–90
   identifying causes of differences in market share of, 89
   opportunity maps, 93–94
   peer groups, 92–93, 96
   prioritizing, 90
   sales force and, 85
   sales plays for types of, 92–93
Millennials, 164

INDEX

mobilizers, 77–80, 131–132
  decreasing individual risk for, 135–136
  equipping for effectiveness, 137–138
  increasing perceived rewards for, 136–137
  motivating, 135–137
  tools for, 135
motivation
  of buyers, 14–16
  of mobilizers, 135–137
  of salespeople, 113–114, 149–160

Narus, James A., 115–125
network performance, 110–111
noncash incentives, 159
nonstrategic purchases, 116–118, 125

opportunity maps, 93–94
organizational climate
  changing, 105–109
  insight selling and, 103
organizational culture, 12, 111, 166–167
outsourcing, of sales function, 49–50

peer groups, 92–93, 96
performance management, 95–96, 104
power bases, 9–14
price competition, 102, 106
price concessions, 117–118
pricing, 27
principal-agent theory, 151–152
products
  benefits of, 14–15
  marketing of, 28
promotion costs, 27–28

psychological intelligence, 3, 18–21
purchase decisions. *See* buying process
purchasers, 7, 8. *See also* buyers
purchasing managers, 116–119

quarterly business reviews, 120

Rackham, Neil, 23–44
ratcheting quotas, 150, 151
resource allocation, 59–61, 91–92, 95
revenue targets, 42
reward power, 10
reward systems, 42. *See also* compensation
Roberge, Mark, 139–148
route sales, 149

salaries, 152, 164
sales audits, 19–21
sales calls, productive, 18–19
sales contests, 144–145
sales cycle, lengthening of, 101
sales department
  budget, 27–28
  relationship between marketing and, 23–44, 96–98, 138
sales force
  account managers, 61–62
  business growth and, 52–58
  colocation of, with marketers, 37
  compensation for, 113–114, 139–168
  complaints by, 149
  in declining companies, 62–65
  declining size of, 167–168
  diminishing role of, 164–165
  distribution of, 91–92
  downsizing, 62–64

INDEX

feedback from, 37
four factors for a successful, 48
high-performing, 69-70, 72-82
judgment and creativity of, 102, 103, 105-109, 112-113
latitude for, 106
listening to, 19-21
in mature companies, 59-62
micromarkets and, 85
motivations of, 113-114, 149-160
outsourcing of, 49-50
performance management, 95-96
quality and attitude of, 164
ROI on, 57
size of, 50-52, 54-58
solution selling and, 67-82
as source of innovation, 167
specialization of, 52-53
in start-up companies, 48-52
structure of, and business life cycle, 45-65
supporting, 93-94, 103, 107-109
talent development, 98, 112-114
sales funnel, 39, 41, 106, 107-108
sales machine, 101-114
 judgment-oriented, 105
 process-driven, 102, 103, 105
sales managers
 facilitation by, 109-111
 importance of, 166
 informal communication by, 111
 long-term focus of, 112
 as peer-level guides, 108-109
 role of, 109-112
sales metrics, 42-43, 103
sales opportunities
 aligning sales coverage with, 91-92
 creating sales plays for types of, 92-93
 data analysis to identify, 97
 prioritizing, 73-74

sales presentations, 71-73
sales quotas
 cumulative, 157
 gaming of, 152-153, 155-156
 ratcheting, 150, 151
 setting and adjusting, 156, 159-160, 162
sales territories, 61
sales tools, 135
Schmidt, Karl, 127-138
self-interest, 3, 14
sellers
 adaptable, 102
 perceptions about, 16-18
 "shared learning," 133-134
Sinha, Prabhakant, 45-65
Skeptics, 77-78, 79
social media analytics, 97, 133
solution selling, 67-82, 165-166
SonoSite, 49-50
specialization, of sales force, 52-53
spreadsheet coaching, 108
stakeholders, 104
 consensus among multiple, 127-138
 identifying common ground among, 132-134
 types of, 74-80
start-up companies
 key stages for, 140-145
 sales force for, 48-52
 tech, 167
status power, 10, 11-12
strategic purchases, 116
suppliers, misunderstanding of customers by, 116-118
sustainable growth plan, 143-145

talent development, 98, 112-114
"Talkers," 76, 77, 79
"Teachers," 76, 77-78, 79

tech start-ups, 167
tiebreaker selling, 115–125
Toman, Nicholas, 67–82, 101–114
turnarounds, 62–65

undefined relationship, between sales and marketing, 29, 34, 35
users, 7, 8

value selling, 121
vendors, perceptions about, 16–18

watercooler effect, 153
win labs, 94
Wouters, Marc, 115–125

Zoltners, Andris A., 45–65, 161–168

Invaluable insights
always at your fingertips

With an All-Access subscription to *Harvard Business Review*, you'll get so much more than a magazine.

Exclusive online content and tools
you can put to use today

My Library, your personal workspace for sharing, saving, and organizing HBR.org articles and tools

---

Unlimited access to more than 4,000 articles in the *Harvard Business Review* archive

---

Subscribe today at hbr.org/subnow

The most important management ideas all in one place.

We hope you enjoyed this book from *Harvard Business Review*. Now you can get even more with HBR's 10 Must Reads Boxed Set. From books on leadership and strategy to managing yourself and others, this 6-book collection delivers articles on the most essential business topics to help you succeed.

HBR's 10 Must Reads Series

The definitive collection of ideas and best practices on our most sought-after topics from the best minds in business.

- Change Management
- Collaboration
- Communication
- Emotional Intelligence
- Innovation
- Leadership
- Making Smart Decisions
- Managing Across Cultures
- Managing People
- Managing Yourself
- Strategic Marketing
- Strategy
- Teams
- The Essentials

hbr.org/mustreads

Buy for your team, clients, or event.
Visit hbr.org/bulksales for quantity discount rates.

Printed in the USA
CPSIA information can be obtained
at www.ICGtesting.com
JSHW082308090224
57034JS00002B/25